Rebecca Plett
Psalm 46:10

DEPRESSION HAS A BIG VOICE
MAKE YOURS BIGGER!

REBECCA PLATT

WestBow Press
A DIVISION OF THOMAS NELSON
& ZONDERVAN

Copyright © 2021 Rebecca Platt.

All rights reserved. No part of this book may be used or reproduced by any means, graphic, electronic, or mechanical, including photocopying, recording, taping or by any information storage retrieval system without the written permission of the author except in the case of brief quotations embodied in critical articles and reviews.

WestBow Press books may be ordered through booksellers or by contacting:

WestBow Press
A Division of Thomas Nelson & Zondervan
1663 Liberty Drive
Bloomington, IN 47403
www.westbowpress.com
844-714-3454

Because of the dynamic nature of the Internet, any web addresses or links contained in this book may have changed since publication and may no longer be valid. The views expressed in this work are solely those of the author and do not necessarily reflect the views of the publisher, and the publisher hereby disclaims any responsibility for them.

Any people depicted in stock imagery provided by Getty Images are models, and such images are being used for illustrative purposes only. Certain stock imagery © Getty Images.

Scripture taken from the NEW AMERICAN STANDARD BIBLE®, Copyright © 1960, 1962, 1963, 1968, 1971, 1972, 1973, 1975, 1977, 1995 by The Lockman Foundation. Used by permission. www.Lockman.org

ISBN: 978-1-6642-3233-4 (sc)
ISBN: 978-1-6642-3232-7 (hc)
ISBN: 978-1-6642-3234-1 (e)

Library of Congress Control Number: 2021908270

Print information available on the last page.

WestBow Press rev. date: 6/21/2021

Anyone can struggle with depression, anxiety, and other low mood disorders. However, everyone can learn to manage these disorders if given the correct tools. This book does that and much more.

CONTENTS

Acknowledgments xi
Author's Note xiii
Introduction xvii

PART ONE

Day 1	The Big Question. Is Depression Sin? 1
Day 2	Does God Send Depression? 4
Day 3	What Depression Is Not 7
Day 4	There Is No Shame 10
Day 5	Admitting to Depression 13
Day 6	Hope Is the First Step 16
Day 7	Stay the Course 19
Day 8	Cry Out for Healing 21
Day 9	Depression Has a Big Voice. Make Yours Bigger! 24
Day 10	Talk Back to Your Depression 27
Day 11	Depression and Illness 29
Day 12	What You Don't Monitor You Can't Change 32
Day 13	God Is with You on This Journey 35
Day 14	When Depression Has You Facedown 38
Day 15	More on the Woman Bent Over 41
Day 16	Acting as If 44
Day 17	Faith and Trust: The Difference 47
Day 18	How Depression Steals Our Time 50
Day 19	Grace and Medication 53
Day 20	Don't Compare and Then Despair 56
Day 21	Our Triggers Are Unique 59

Day 22	When You Just Want to Be Left Alone	62
Day 23	When It's Just Too Much	65
Day 24	Spiritual Depression	68
Day 25	Keep God in the Equation	71
Day 26	Why Forgiveness Matters	74
Day 27	Preparing for Depression	77
Day 28	Living below the Clouds	80
Day 29	The Woman in Barnes and Noble	83
Day 30	Lower Your Expectations	86
Day 31	Know Who and Whose You Are	89
Day 32	Anxiety and Decision-Making	92
Day 33	Were You Born Too Old?	95
Day 34	If We Were Having Coffee	98
Day 35	Changed Relationships	101
Day 36	Healthy Relationships	103
Day 37	What Is a Good Friendship?	105
Day 38	Relationships: The Sequel	108
Day 39	Who Is Writing Your Story?	111
Day 40	Why Boundaries Are Good	114
Day 41	Statistics Are Not Your Destiny	117
Day 42	Don't Ignore Your Feelings	120
Day 43	Are You Taking Vitamin G?	123
Day 44	Loneliness	126
Day 45	The CETH Program	129
Day 46	Getting a Grip on Anger	132
Day 47	Sadness	135
Day 48	Unrelenting Fear	138
Day 49	That Green-Eyed Monster	141
Day 50	Whose Guilt Is It Really?	144
Day 51	Distraction Is a Wonderful Thing	147
Day 52	What Do Your Words Say about You?	150
Day 53	Think about What You Are Thinking About	153
Day 54	You've Got to "Move It, Move It, Move It"	156
Day 55	The Scourge of Mindless Sitting	159

Day 56   A Surprise Attack 162
Day 57   David, Goliath, and Depression 166
Day 58   The Best Self-Help Book 169
Day 59   Prayer: Easier Than You Think 172
Day 60   Unpack Your Suitcase 175

PART TWO
The Toolbox 179
Distraction Ideas (no particular order) 203

ACKNOWLEDGMENTS

I would like to thank everyone who has ever breathed Jesus into my life, including former pastors, Sunday school teachers, Bible teachers, strangers, and books that have inspired me and become my friends.

Thank you to the WestBow staff who put up with my constant questions and, at times, my frustrations.

To those I told I was writing a book about depression who never blinked an eye, thank you for not fainting.

To my son, Mark, and daughter, Shannon, who have been with me on this journey to wholeness even though they didn't always know it at the time. I respect and admire you both beyond what any mother could expect. You are both inspirations to me.

Mostly, to the love of my life, my husband. You never once raised an eyebrow when I told you I was really going to write a book. You were my biggest cheerleader and encouraged me every step of the way. But that's not what I thank you for the most.

I have often said that pretty much everything I know about God's love I've learned through your love for me. You never once criticized me or made me feel bad for struggling with depression. Instead, you have just loved me.

This book is for you. Thank you for being my best friend and hero and a living example of Christ's love.

And finally, thank You, God, for giving me this call and for leading every step of the way. We did it, didn't we? I think I just might have made You smile.

AUTHOR'S NOTE

When I was a little girl, if someone told me I would someday write a book, I wouldn't have been overly surprised. Not because I had any particular leanings in that direction but because I've always had a good imagination.

As a little girl, I would play in the woods and design rooms from branches and twigs. I would pretend to live happily in my woodsy home because it was the only place I felt at peace. I would spend hours outside, making up a fantasy world where mothers and fathers loved each other and hugged their children a lot.

Words were always important to me. I found, and still find, words fascinating and full of promise. I would make up stories for my children. I wrote an entire daily vacation Bible school program once.

A number of years ago I even started writing a novel about a young Christian woman in the South who is naive and full of wonder until events conspire to change all that. It's about a devastating fire, a love lost, a love found, and secrets that surprise the reader in the end. I'm still working on that one.

When I finally realized God was whispering in my ear to write a book, I assumed it was the book I had already started. Never assume with God. Anyway, I continued to write that novel, and it was a going great until …

God made it clear that was *not* the book He was talking about. So, of course, I started another one. Right?

Apparently, that wasn't the book He was talking about either. I really liked that one as well. It's about a young woman who finds a mysterious box in rest stop bathroom and what the note inside reads.

No, God was making it clear He wanted me to write about the one subject I didn't want to be in print with my name on it: depression.

As a public speaker, I had addressed this issue with many audiences over the years. I had taught Bible classes. I had been a hospital chaplain and witnessed suffering up close. I'd been there when family members were taken off life support. I had spoken at workshops and retreats so I was used to being in the public eye, but this was entirely different. This time, my words would live on. They would be in print, where anyone could tear me and my words apart. I wasn't ready for that.

But I wrote anyway because I could do nothing else. That's what happens when God gets a grip on us. I started writing on and off. I liked the book, but something just wasn't right.

After prayer and hard thinking, I came to the conclusion the book needed to be in a devotional form. I got back to the writing. Then COVID-19 hit, and for me, that was a green light.

Everything was on hold anyway, so I pushed through to the end of the book. My eyes burned out of their sockets on some days. But I finished it. And you, dear reader, now have it in your hands.

It's a not a perfect book. I'm sure not everyone will agree with everything I've written. That's OK. I don't agree with everything other authors write either. We can learn from those with whom we disagree as much as we can from those with whom we do agree.

I have done my homework. The number of books I've read over the years about this particular subject is exhausting. I try to stay abreast of all the latest research as well. This book wasn't written on a whim or without due diligence.

I am not a doctor or a mental health professional. Neither was Jesus, and yet He spoke words of encouragement. He spoke honestly. He spoke directly. I have tried to emulate that style throughout this book, knowing, of course, that it pales in significance.

I refer to my own struggles in this book without reservation or apology. I know what depression feels like and looks like. I have witnessed how depression can suck the joy out of life. I have witnessed it in countless others and have also known the personal frustration of feeling there was nothing I could do for them.

When I began writing, I had no conscious idea I had actually developed tools for managing my depression. I just knew I was getting better, but I hadn't connected the dots. Once I realized there were certain coping mechanisms I was using over and over through the years and that they worked, the toolbox came into existence.

The first part of this book is a sixty-day devotional. The second part is the toolbox.

I told myself if even one person is helped from this book, I will have accomplished what I set out to do. Well, even before this book went to press, it happened.

I asked someone from a professional online writing group of which I am a member to read this book and do a minor edit. We had actually talked months earlier, and she had been such an encourager. After I sent her the book to read, she emailed me and told me what had happened that day on her end. Apparently, I had shared something from the book that really hit home for her, and she told me it started her on the road to recovery.

As I read her words, I teared up. I couldn't believe God was using the book before it was even printed.

The point of that story is to encourage you and remind you that we have no idea how we can influence others by what we say or write. Even the most casual remark can make a difference if the Holy Spirit is behind it. Don't ever underestimate how God is working in the strangest ways at times and at the strangest times.

Do I have trouble with depression or anxiety now? It would

be less than honest to say I don't. Anxiety has reared its nasty head this past year due to the COVID-19 virus, the elections, my health, and this book. For one short period, I did go back on the most minor dose of an antidepressants to get me over the hump. (The doctor said it wasn't even a therapeutic dose, so who knows.) But at no time over the past twenty years have I struggled with a case of clinical depression. I have limped along more than once but haven't fallen. God has kept my feet on solid ground.

I could write another whole book about all the circumstances, scriptures, prayers, and people who came together and inspired the words in this book.

Don't give up. True clinical depression can be a distant memory for you, just like it is for me.

God bless.

You can let me know your thoughts at faithsighanddiy.com/underhiswings.

INTRODUCTION

Depression can be likened to a roller-coaster ride that is so terrifying and has so many twists, turns, and upside downs that you can't wait to get off. And you certainly don't ever want to take this particular ride again. This book is written for those who have suffered or are suffering mild to moderate depression, with or without anxiety. It can also be used for low moods in general. (https://www.nimh.nih.gov/health/topics/depression/).

Christians, too, are subject to mental health issues. But we have a Savior to cling to for, *"He brought me up out of the pit of destruction, out of the mud; And He set my feet on a rock, making my footsteps firm."* Psalms 40:2. I don't know how I would've have come through some situations without God keeping my feet from slipping off that rock.

While this book does not address severe forms of mental illness, it can still contribute constructively to overall good mental health. Don't change any treatment plans without consulting with your doctor, and please feel free to share this book with him or her. I am not a medical doctor nor a medical health professional. If you have any concerns, consult your primary care physician.

Dorothy Rowe, in her classic book *Depression*, describes depression as a prison. She makes the point that it doesn't really matter how we ended up in our prison; the first matter of business is getting out. Imagine yourself in that prison. What if, as you sat that prison cell, you had the tools to open the door the whole time? This devotional will provide you with these tools.

You may wonder why I chose sixty days as opposed to, say,

thirty or ninety. Ninety days, when you're feeling miserable, is just way too long. Thirty days is not long enough to establish good practices. Sixty days seemed just right. If you are faithfully using these tools, you will feel some improvement in those sixty days. The more the tools become habitual, the better you will feel.

You will probably find that a particular tool strikes an immediate responsive chord. Others, not so much. This will depend on where you are on your personal journey, how much you know about depression (Read about depression when you feel better, as forewarned is forearmed) and how hard you are willing to work.

Some of what I suggest may seem contradictory. That's because managing depression is often about the timing. For example, sometimes it's good to rest sometimes it's good to be active. Sometimes it's good to really examine your depression and look for causes; sometimes it's not.

For the information in this book to really work, it needs to be carefully *read*, thoughtfully *pondered*, and consistently *practiced*. One approach will work one day but seem less effective the next. Our behaviors, routines, words, and thoughts have become habits. Change takes time and is just plain hard work. Plus, there are many ways we get in the way of our own recovery.

This book will not address the various types of medication. Whether you should take them or not is between you and your doctor. Just remember there is no shame in taking medication for a while. There is no shame if you must always take medication. And don't pride yourself if you never have to take medication at all. It's not a contest.

Studies do indeed show a chemical imbalance in the brains of those who are depressed, but I'm unaware of any research that states which came first, the chemical imbalance or the depression. However, the imbalance still needs to be addressed and normalized through medication, counseling, behavior modification or a combination of all three.

There is a way to break free from your prison. Your fluctuating moods don't have to be in control.

I am no stronger, braver, or smarter than anyone else. I was reading my Bible. I was praying. I was an active member of a church. I had a loving and understanding husband, great children, and good friends. And yet depression, and the stigma surrounding it, had me in its prison for many years. I, like many, carried my burden of depression well, hiding it behind my smiles.

So, when you read this book remember the advice has to be adapted and used within the parameters of your unique circumstances. When I suggest, for example, to get up and make your bed in the morning but you work a second or third shift, you would modify that to your particular schedule. The point is to get moving.

Imagine going to the doctor, for example, and complaining of a backache every time you pick up anything more than twenty pounds. Their advice? "Then quit picking up anything that weighs more than twenty pounds." In other words, if it hurts, don't do it. Commonsense, practical advice. In regard to depression, it might be, "I feel anxious when I do so-and-so." Advice? "Limit the so-and-sos."

As you read this book and think these ideas sound too simple for how bad you feel, try them anyway. Every constructive step you take paves the way for the next one. After a while, those steps become a clear path to your journey's end.

Most of the time there are logical and knowable reasons why we get depressed. But there are times when depression seems to strike without warning. Don't panic if you can't figure it out. Maybe there isn't that one thing you can uncover right now but you might look back in a few months and determine the cause

There have been rare occasions when I didn't have a clue either. Sometimes we can drive ourselves to the edge looking for answers. On those rare occasions, I simply picked up my tools and put one foot in front of the other until I was better. I'm still picking up my tools.

I've been on the depression roller-coaster ride. I've experienced the up and down and all-around of this not-so-amusing trip. I've taken the pills and counseled with the professionals. And I'm here to tell you that you can beat depression. You can send it to a corner and keep it there. Give it an indefinite time-out.

Finally, I wrote this book because I couldn't *not* write this book. For years, God persisted, and I balked. I have a deep passion for helping anyone who deals with this mind-sucking, joy-robbing illness. I know what depression feels like, and I wouldn't wish it on anyone.

You can manage your depression, your anxiety, your moods.

Depression may be a giant but it's nothing against a Spirit-powered small stone rocketed from a slingshot by a person of faith.

I like to mentally place myself in scenes in the Bible. Try to put yourself in some of the scenes, like maybe the woman bent over from a long-standing illness. Try to imagine what it was like to be her, looking down at the dirt all the time. When people walked by, you inhaled the dust from their sandals. The only time you saw the sky was if you were on your back. People quit trying to converse with you because it was too difficult. After a while, you were unseen.

Imagine when you hear the news that Jesus is coming. Imagine your excitement. "Will He heal me? Can I even be healed?" you ask yourself. You are scared and excited at the same time. Then, there He is! At least there His robe is. You can't see His face, but you do hear His voice, and it's much different than you thought it would be. It's not soft, but it is warm, authoritative, powerful. Your heart beats wildly as you approach ...

I like to imagine that God assigns a box to each of us when we are born. Mine is painted white over black and distressed to reveal the first coat. The handles and hinges are gold, and the velvet lining is the softest shade of blue-green. (I love all things DIY. Can you tell?)

When we our born, our boxes are filled with our unique talents, gifts, and abilities. I imagine the day when I'm standing at the gates of heaven, and Jesus is there holding my box. Is it empty or full? I watch Jesus open my box with a smile on my face, and tears streaming down my cheeks, knowing He will find it empty. (*I get weepy every time I think of it and, yes, I know Jesus already knows the box is empty but this is my story.*)

This book is the next step in emptying my box and hopefully encouraging you to empty yours.

God bless you richly as you read this book.

PART ONE

PART ONE

DAY 1

THE BIG QUESTION. IS DEPRESSION SIN?

> All have sinned and fallen short of the glory of God.
> —Romans 3:23

Is depression sin? Absolutely, unequivocally, *no*.

There are hundreds of Bible verses that address our moods, and nowhere do any of them suggest that our moods or emotions are sin. Even the verse "Be angry and yet, do not sin; do not let the sun go down on your anger" (Ephesians 4:26) does not say the emotion of anger is a sin. It's what we do with the anger that matters.

Many Christians do not view depression as the serious illness it is. That's because they don't consider it an illness; they consider it a sin. I am always surprised that many Christians have been so slow to understand this. The research is out there. But maybe I shouldn't be.

The subject of depression is rarely addressed from the pulpit even though a large number of the congregation is or has been affected by this illness or knows someone who is. When is the last time you heard an intelligent, compassionate sermon about depression? They are few and far between, and it's a rare minister who will tackle the subject.

Why is that?

I would suggest it's because pastors may be uncomfortable

addressing it due to their lack of medical knowledge. But the subject could still be addressed. Also, it just might hit a little too close to home.

Rare is the pastor or religious leader who admits to struggling with depression, although many famous ones, including Charles Spurgeon, Beth Moore, and John Piper, have. The subject is shoved under the sanctified carpet with all the other issues the church doesn't address.

Jesus, while praying in the garden of Gethsemane, suffered the worst kind of depression, and while our depression cannot be compared to His, I'll bet there are many people who read that passage and say to themselves, "I feel just like that!" I know I have.

But are there cases where sin can cause depression? Of course. Anytime we continuously engage in an activity we know is sin, we open the door to depression. No Christian knowingly engaged in constant sin can help but have their mental health challenged in some way.

Christians who continue with activities that are outside God's will often pile up heaps of guilt on themselves. The higher the piles get, the harder it is to get out from under them. And the more guilt they feel, the more Satan has an opportunity to take their guilt and turn it into depression and anxiety. Satan loves for us to feel guilty. He knows that guilt creates a chasm between us and God. Think Judas.

But depression, left unchecked, can also *cause* us to sin. People will engage in all kinds of self-destructive behaviors to feel better—alcohol abuse, drug abuse, promiscuity, gambling, overeating, undereating, and more. The sad truth is that any and all of these behaviors will only exacerbate the symptoms.

We can get caught up in sinful behavior easily because we just want the pain to go away. Because we are trying to alleviate the pain, we walk closer to sin's tentacles. What starts out as only questionable behavior turns into a dance with the devil. Eventually, we walk too close to the edge of the pit and fall in.

So, let's put this to rest. Depression itself is not a sin, although sin may have prompted it, and sin may be the outcome if self-destructive behaviors are resorted to.

When you are depressed, do you find yourself tempted to engage in sinful activities to alleviate the pain?

Will you create a plan that will help you avoid them?

DAY 2

DOES GOD SEND DEPRESSION?

> Rabbi, who sinned, this man or his parents, that he was born blind? Neither this man nor his parents have sinned.
> —John 9:1–12

If we believe in the omniscience, omnipresence, and omnipotence of God, we also have to believe God that could have prevented our depression, no matter what caused it. And yet Christians do suffer from depression. It is not a lack of faith. It is that we live in a fallen world and are as subject to its trials, difficulties, and depression as anyone else is.

Our chemistry is complex.

Our lives are complex.

Our history is complex.

God could change all the bad things that happen to us; this is true. The fact that He doesn't is also true. Countless authors have tried to explain this. It's the leading reason many people refuse to embrace any kind of faith. I certainly won't try to answer the subject of suffering and pain. But if you want a biblical account of someone who did challenge God about these issues and how God responded, read Job 38–41 and the short book of Habakkuk.

And frankly, I understand it. I understand that confusion. I honestly do get why some people have a hard time believing in a loving God when so much evil prevails.

But I also know that when in my deepest pit, I felt God's loving arms preventing me from making an eternal mistake for what was a temporary condition. All I know is that I experienced His rescuing love. I don't know what else to say.

Do I believe God sent all my depressive episodes? No. But some? Quite possibly.

There might be those rare times when God uses depression to discipline us. It is meant to stretch us, grow us, and reveal to us the areas of our lives that may need some scrutiny. We could call those times "spiritual" depressions. (Spiritual depression is discussed later.) The symptoms are much the same. I would add that often they overlap.

Any depression, no matter the trigger, can certainly cause us to question the basic tenets of our faith. It's hard to read our Bibles and pray when we feel so disconnected from God and ourselves. We are so confused we don't even know what to pray about.

So, yes, it is biblical that God may well discipline us—at times through depression. But discipline generally occurs because we have knowingly engaged in activities that have not been stamped with God's approval and are a result of disobedience.

God's discipline, however, should not lead to clinical depression if handled correctly. If it does, there are probably other issues at play. I think Jonah, for example, had some other issues, like pride, going on when God disciplined him. Like Jonah, we can accept God's discipline and go on from there, or we can sweat it out under the hot sun with no shade.

But then there are some people who want to believe that God is always behind their depression. That makes some sort of convoluted sense.

After all, if they can blame God for their depression, they don't have to accept any responsibility for it, do they? It's all on Him. After all, if God sent it, He can just take it away. So, they suffer through it and claim martyrdom rather than do any work to get better.

Charles Spurgeon never blamed God for his depression. He

dealt with it when it flared up and kept right on preaching, teaching, and writing. Many spiritual leaders have been there, done that. God always wants us to win our battles. If we find ourselves in this battle of depression, God will hold up our hands until our battle is over, just as Aaron and Hur did with Moses (Exodus 17:12).

Defeat will never come from God's hands, only our own.

Have you ever wondered if God sent your depression?
Have you ever blamed God for your depression?

DAY 3
WHAT DEPRESSION IS NOT

> You, O, Lord keep my lamp burning; my
> God turns my darkness into light.
> —Psalm 18:28

The word *depression* has come to mean something different than its definition according to the National Mental Health Institute (NIMH). (https://www.nimh.nih.gov/health/topics/depression/)

People throw the word around carelessly these days, calling fleeting uncomfortable emotions caused by temporary situations *depression*. "I'm so depressed because …" As soon as the situation improves, so does their depression. That's not clinical depression; that's the ordinary fallout of some discouraging days.

Depression, otherwise known as major depressive disorder or clinical depression, is a common and serious mood disorder. To be diagnosed with depression, the majority of symptoms must be present for at least two weeks. While more and more people are being diagnosed with depression, I believe there are many more who are suffering in silence.

Depression is more than just sadness—although it may certainly include feelings of sadness. It is a *profound* sense of sadness where you feel hopeless and discouraged about pretty much everything. You don't see the faintest glimmer of light at the end of the tunnel. Not even a tiny little ember.

A depressed person can be depressed independent of a situation. My life was wonderful, yet I was depressed. This is true of many. Depressed people are unable to experience joy. It completely eludes them. Joy in their lives is a distant memory.

When we're only sad, we can still enjoy a good TV show or movie, or a book, or friends. These activities take our mind off our sadness. With depression, we can't concentrate on a show or a book, and we don't want anyone around. Sadness doesn't generally affect our eating or sleeping habits—depression does.

Clinical depression impacts every part of a person's life. True clinical depression is a whole-body illness. More and more research proves that depression affects many parts of our bodies and can make us physically unwell. It is now believed that our gut health and inflammation have a lot to do with our mental health, possibly even being a cause for some people. Much of our serotonin is produced in our gut. What a relief it would be to know that it might not all be in our heads.

Depression always has a price.

In the Gospels, we read about Peter and Judas. Both betrayed Jesus, but only one killed himself. The following is only my theory, but I think you will get my logic. Peter was like that person you know who is rambunctious and loud but endearing at the same time. Know what I mean? I get the sense he drew people to him. But Judas?

Judas probably wasn't popular. He was a loner. He handled the money, which means he was probably good with numbers. But like most accountants, he was probably quieter and more task oriented. An accountant's job requires it. (I know. I'm married to one.)

After Peter betrayed Jesus, I think he might have gone to the other disciples and told them what he had done. They probably chastised him, but because they had come to expect his brash behavior (the disciples still didn't believe that Jesus would actually die anyway), they overlooked it. What Peter did was horrific, but he and the disciples probably did not see it as a permanent mistake. So I'm thinking Peter probably felt some sense of relief.

Not so with Judas. Judas *did* try to give back his dirty money but was told, "Too late." I believe Judas, probably always skirting depression anyway, now experienced the hallmark symptoms of depression, helplessness and hopelessness. Without someone to talk to, going back to my theory that he was probably a loner, he felt lost. He took the only action he could think of.

Two different men. Two different betrayals. Two very big sins.

One survived and went on to become a pillar of the New Testament church; the other hung himself.

Judas's legacy? The world would always remember him as a traitor, and his name would always be spoken with contempt.

Depression has a price.

What price are you paying for your depression?
Would you like to pay less?

DAY 4
THERE IS NO SHAME

> Those who look to Him are radiant, and
> their faces shall never be ashamed.
> —Psalm 34:5

Some people in Christian circles would suggest you should feel a lot of shame for your depression.

They are quick to judge and quick to condemn. They do so because they have never been there; they simply don't believe it's a real illness, or they pridefully think they would never succumb to it. I would kindly suggest that a person who doesn't understand depression or anxiety is a person who has never allowed themselves to feel very deeply.

These same people would never suggest that PTSD is shameful. But, much like victims of PTSD, people who suffer from depression or anxiety often have a traumatic history as well. When it happens at a young age, our brains are almost hardwired to react to life stressors with impaired mental abilities. Even if you are not the actual victim, the stress of family violence has an impact.

Jesus did not shame the woman caught in adultery any more than the men. They were both at fault, but you notice His harshest words were for those who had abused her and heaped shame on her. Jesus saw them as the instigators.

Why?

Because they were laying their own shame on her. They were acting as though they had done nothing wrong, much like the Pharisees. They were hypocritical, and if there was one attribute Jesus addressed more often than others, it was hypocrisy.

Very often, the people who criticize those with mental illness have their own issues. The difference? No one else knows about them. They are clean on the outside.

Isn't that what Jesus said about the Pharisees? "You are clean on the outside only" (Matthew 23:25).

If you have run into Christians who belittled or made you feel shame for being depressed, listen to me.

Can you think of a single verse that suggests God is ashamed of you when you are sick? You can't, because there aren't any. Your depression and your anxiety are illnesses as well. However, just like with the majority of more acceptable illnesses, there are things you can do to be healed.

Are there some behaviors in your life that will need to change? Probably.

But, praise God, He loves us in our weakness just like He loves us in our strength. You don't have to hang your head in shame.

I love what John Lockley writes in *A Practical Guidebook for the Depressed Christian*, "Being depressed is bad enough by itself; but being a depressed Christian is worse."

I came across a wonderful saying the other day. I don't know its origin. "Shame off you. Grace on you." Isn't that wonderful?

Depression is hard enough without adding unneeded shame to the mix. And by the way, it's quite possible to be in the center of God's will while also being in the center of a storm. Being depressed doesn't necessarily mean you are outside God's will any more than a broken leg does.

Ignore those armchair doctors. It's amazing how many people would never think to add their two cents about someone's medical diagnosis, but are experts when it comes to depression.

When you are better, you can educate them a little if the occasion arises.

Until then, remind yourself of how much God loves you right now—right in the middle of your depression.

Have you encountered people who have shamed you because of your depression?

How can you handle it in the future?

DAY 5

ADMITTING TO DEPRESSION

> You are my hiding place. You will protect me from trouble and surround me with songs of deliverance.
> —Psalm 32:7

If you are looking for certain passages in the Bible that mention that so-and-so was depressed, you are not going to find them.

Nowhere does the Bible say, for example, that Moses suffered from depression. But did men and women in the Bible show symptoms that today would definitely result in such a diagnosis? Yes. Let's look at some other examples first.

How about Abraham Lincoln? He suffered what he described as severe melancholy. Letters from his friends stated he was the most depressed person they'd ever seen.

Winston Churchill used writing and painting to keep the "black dog of depression at bay."

Martin Luther King Jr. suffered as well. It is not well known but Martin Luther King Jr., twice attempted to commit suicide before the age of thirteen. It has also been reported that his staff even tried to get him psychiatric treatment, shortly before he was assassinated.

For more modern-day examples, there is Katy Perry, who quite recently shared her struggles with depression. Lady Gaga has admitted to it, as have Kristen Bell and Bruce Springsteen.

Dwayne "the Rock" Johnson has opened up about his depression recently. Being famous makes no difference.

Now let's look at those examples from scripture. Their symptoms could be a dip in their emotional or mental state, or it could reflect long-term illness: Moses (Numbers 11:14), Hannah, (1 Samuel 1:7, 16), Jeremiah (Jeremiah 20:14–18), and of course David and many of the psalmists. Martin Lloyd-Jones even suggests that Timothy suffered from a nearly paralyzing anxiety.

Now, you may be saying, "Yes, but these people weren't like the rest of us. They were heroes." Well, they weren't heroes until they became heroes, right? They battled their depression and other mental disorders long before their names were recorded in scripture.

Before we can heal from depression, we have to see depression as something more than an illness that strikes other people and not us, especially we people of faith. Because unless we understand that, we will ignore our symptoms because we are ashamed to admit them.

The other danger lies in how we might perceive our spirituality. We will try to find the cause by scrutinizing our relationship with God and coming to the false belief that our depression or anxiety is the result of a spiritual problem. This makes us feel guilty and draws us away from God rather than closer to God.

If ever there was a time to draw near to God, it's when we're battling this illness. While depression can have serious consequences in our spiritual lives, it is not necessarily caused by problems in our spiritual lives.

The more people admit to depression and anxiety, the more likely some of the stigma will be removed, but there are still very few people who don't feel embarrassed and ashamed when acknowledging their struggles. I find it amazing that in this day and age, when we know so much about mental issues, we are still so hesitant to admit to it.

While writing this book, I, too, worried, *What will people think of me? Will they question my spirituality?* It helped knowing I'm in good company with King David, who wrote, "I waited for the LORD: He inclined to me and heard my cry ... He drew me out of the miry blog and set my feet upon a rock, making my step secure" (Psalm 40:1–3).

Read the psalms because they often express despair, discouragement, anxiety, and depression. They can become our prayer when we can't find the words.

You are not alone. Many have been here before; many are here now. But God is faithful if you reach out your hand to Him.

Can you admit to your depression?
Can you trust God to deliver you?

DAY 6
HOPE IS THE FIRST STEP

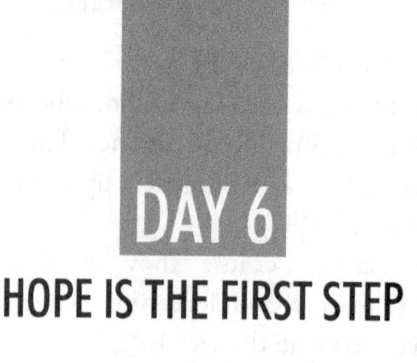

I will hope in Him.
—Job 13:15

Depression robs us of the ability to see beyond our own hurt and pain. In other words, it robs us of hope.

I know a number of people who have struggled with depression. While I might offer varying kinds of help as the circumstances indicate, the one help I can always offer is hope, because hope is never in short supply.

Hope that we can and will get better is like the fuel we put in our engines. Without it, we aren't going anywhere.

Every heroic story I've read about a person overcoming great odds boils down to this one word, *hope*—hope that they will find their way out of the woods, hope that they will stay afloat on a raft until help comes, hope that someone will rescue them from captivity.

If we are to break those chains that keep us under a dark cloud, we must cling to hope.

"'For I know the plans I have for you,' declares the LORD, 'plans to proper you and not to harm you, plans to give you hope and a future'" (Jeremiah 29:11).

God indeed has plans for you. He knows what those plans are, and they are meant to give you hope and a future. That future is full of joy, and God has those plans all laid out for you. All you have to do is keep moving to that future and to those plans.

You will get better. Along that journey, hope is the one constant you can count on. If you let hope slip through your fingers, your journey will take longer.

Depression is not hopeless; it just feels that way.

That's why it's so important to tell yourself you are getting better every day.

But hope isn't hope unless we put it into practice. And some of the ways we do that are using the word, speaking the word, and embracing what the word means.

What is hope?

Biblical hope is the confident expectation that what God has promised, He will deliver. And God has promised us so much. Unlike most of us, God never breaks a promise. You can even remind Him of those promises. I often have. So did King David and others.

We aren't telling God something He doesn't know. We are claiming something He has promised.

There are days when hope is the only thing you can cling to. Let hope grab your hand as you take the next step. Let hope give you sleep and wake you up in the morning.

But without knowing God's promises, hope will be hard to come by. Be sure you know God's promises for you. Claim them. Do an internet search and write down your favorite promises. You will be amazed at the number of them. I often wonder how I would pray and act differently if I knew them so well I could easily call them to my mind.

I have a secret ministry. (It's not secret now, is it?) I type out various scripture verses and paste them to a 2 1/2" x 3 1/2" card that has been covered in pretty scrapbook paper. I encase them in a plastic wrapper. I leave them in bathrooms, at rest stops, in old books I'm getting rid of, and anywhere I can. I know people are hurting, and I pray they are touched when they find one of these little scripture cards. I trust they feel hopeful after they read it.

Embrace hope today. Let hope wrap its arms around you.

Use the word in your speech.

Speak the word. Shout the word.

Write the word and post it where you will see it.

Hope takes some of the sting out of depression. It's like the balm of Gilead to our soul.

Where is your hope today?
Will you believe there is hope for you?

DAY 7
STAY THE COURSE

> He leads me beside the still waters. He restores my soul.
> —Psalm 23:2

Psalm 23 is about being led on a journey. We are symbolically led beside calm waters. Suddenly, we find ourselves in a dark and frightening place. But God is leading there as well.

The psalmist talks about the rod and the staff, sheepherding tools. They have special significance for us on our own journey as well. The staff was used to guide the sheep when they strayed too far or got tangled up in the bushes. The shepherd used the staff to bring that tangled-in-the-bushes sheep back to safety. The rod was then used to gently part the sheep's wool to look for wounds that needed treating.

Today, the staff might well be considered God's Word, which reveals truth to us and guides our journey. The rod could be the Holy Spirit, who opens our wounds to expose them so they can be healed. We might not like seeing our ugly parts, but it's necessary if we are to continue on our journey to wholeness.

The psalmist goes on to say that we don't have to be afraid of evil (depression) because God is with us and is in the business of restoring our soul, even in the presence of our enemies. And we know who that is, don't we?

You are not in this battle alone. God promises to take care

of you today just like a shepherd takes care of his sheep. God is walking through that valley with you, while at the same time walking ahead of you, preparing the way.

He already knows the struggles you will face, the people who might discourage you, the ones who suggest you can't get better. He has already provided the detour around those naysayers. Your only job is to follow Him and to follow Him *daily*.

Staying on the path to recovery means hoping and believing every day that you are getting better. If you are reading this book in order and one day at a time, you are already on day seven of your recovery process. You are already further along the path.

I love to explore unknown trails. If I see a trail ahead of me, I'm on it. I love trails in woods, along the beach, in the park, anywhere. They always remind me that God has a path for me to follow as well. When I was depressed, walking along a trail always made me feel better because I felt it was going somewhere specific. I internalized that to mean I was going to get better if I stayed the course God had prepared for me.

Don't take a detour. Stay on this path to wholeness.

You don't have to know where the path leads. You only have to take it.

Can you picture yourself on this path?
Can you picture God in front of you holding out His hand?

DAY 8

CRY OUT FOR HEALING

> And when Jesus departed from there, two blind men followed Him, crying out and saying, "Son of David, have mercy on us." (Matthew 9:27–30)

This title may seem strange. But depressed people often don't think to ask for healing. I didn't for a long time. I think I know why.

Depression, unlike almost any other illness, is often considered to be self-induced and self-indulgent. Yes, sometimes depressed people contribute to their own mental illness, but people contribute to their own medical illnesses as well. But even if we brought on all our depression, it doesn't mean we can't cry out for healing.

Jesus forgave. Jesus healed. All that was needed was the request.

Some of the most courageous people are those who go about bravely living their lives while at the same time feeling that horrible sense of dread that defies understanding to anyone who has never felt it. Yet they don't cry out because they don't think their illness is even worthy of mention, much less healing. Furthermore, they think it's all their fault.

They feel embarrassed and unworthy of bringing this illness to God for healing because they feel they have brought it on themselves. The cause of the illness has nothing to do with asking for God's help. Would you feel that way about any other illness?

Whether we are completely responsible, somewhat responsible, or not responsible at all, we can bring any illness to God.

There is no barrier to seeking God's help. If we think there is, it's because we put it there.

Don't let feelings of guilt get in your way either. Guilt can be a real stumbling block for someone who is depressed because they are always looking for what they did to bring on their illness.

We can cry out for healing just like these blind men. The blind men knew what they wanted. They wanted to be healed, and they were—immediately.

I'm sure there are people who have been healed from depression immediately too. But for most of us, like for most things in life, it's more of a process. Besides, it takes time to learn principles and coping strategies that will take us through possible future episodes. And even if we never have another one, these same strategies will help us in other areas of our lives.

One of the ways God heals depression is by opening our eyes to our faulty thinking and bad habits. As a general rule, we don't get depressed because we've done all this right. And should it turn out that science will prove depression is only physical, we will still have learned better ways to think and form better habits. And that will serve us well in the future.

God heals through books. I can't tell you the number of times I've randomly picked up a book and read something that literally got me through the day. We don't often think of books as part of the healing process, but they are.

Of course, God also heals through bringing loving and understanding people into our lives. Sometimes they are family, friends, or pastors; often they are complete strangers. Sometimes they are even people we don't particularly like. But they're just the *sandpaper* we need. God has often spoken to me through people I've just met and am not likely to meet again.

Another way God heals is by prompting us to seek medical help. God can heal through medicine. God's healing doesn't have to subscribe to any one method. He can and does heal however He chooses. Don't close the door on any avenue God leads you to pursue just because of what someone might think—or what you might think. Don't be so stubborn you end up making your depression even worse.

One thing is for sure. God doesn't generally heal unless He's invited.

It begins with the asking.

The blind men knew that.

Do you?

Have you prayed for healing?
If so, are you trusting that God is doing just that?

DAY 9

DEPRESSION HAS A BIG VOICE. MAKE YOURS BIGGER!

> Decide for this day whom you will serve, God or man.
> —Joshua 24:15

Preventing a depressive episode is often about the timing. Being proactive and knowing our triggers always proves beneficial, as does knowing we are always making choices, good or bad.

Even today, I had to apply this principle to the writing of this book. I had to motivate myself. I am scared to put this book in print because the pandemic is in full swing. Will people think I am capitalizing on their fear?

Then someone reminded me that the only person who doesn't want me to finish this book is the one filling my minds with these thoughts, Satan. This book has been in the works for years. God knows that, and He's the one I'm accountable to. He is the only one who will be there when I open my box. (See the introduction.) So I made a choice to go ahead, confident that I am following God's call on my life.

Most people don't believe they are always making choices. Ask yourself, Who, other than you, decides to think what you think, say what you say, and do what you do? God does not manipulate your thoughts, words, or actions. You do that. I do that.

DEPRESSION HAS A BIG VOICE

In the book *Man's Search for Meaning*, Holocaust survivor Viktor Frankl wrote, "Everything can be taken from a man but one thing: the last of the human freedoms—to choose one's attitude in any given set of circumstances to choose one's own way."

When you come to that place in your life where, based on the leading of the Holy Spirit, you really believe you are the one deciding where your life is headed, only then will you start to take charge of your life. And the one thing you must learn to do is recognize when depression is making those choices *for* you.

So, how does depression speak?

Often, I found that if I looked back over a period of a few weeks, I could spot those times I let depression make the choices for me. For example, if I indulged in a TV marathon at night while eating junk food when I hadn't purposefully planned to, that meant depression was doing the deciding for me.

If I had a day, however, when after work or on the weekend, I decided that I could watch *some* TV and eat *some* ice cream, then it was me calling the shots. I hope you see the difference. It's all about being aware of who's making the decisions, you or your depression.

I paid attention to the activities of my day.

Depression and anxiety have very loud voices. They are often the loudest voice in the room, even if no one but you hears them. This is a hard concept to explain until you've experienced it. But depression/anxiety does speak. The trick is to recognize its voice and make yours bigger.

And I should add, depression has a veracious appetite as well. It will feed off you until there is nothing left. Keep doing the wrong things, keep thinking the wrong thoughts, keep ignoring your time with God, and you are feeding the monster. But it will die of starvation if it doesn't have food.

Don't be its entrée.

Look back over a recent day and see if you can follow what I mean. I don't know how I figured it out, but I came to the awareness that many of the bad choices I made were choices I wouldn't have made had I *not* been depressed. For me, that led to the theory that depression does have a voice.

It was when I started making my voice louder, empowered by God and His Word, that my depression started to become manageable. The more I felt I was managing it, the more I felt empowered, and the more I felt hope.

Have you ever thought that depression has a voice?
Do you think you can learn to recognize it?

DAY 10
TALK BACK TO YOUR DEPRESSION

"Get behind me Satan! You are a stumbling block to me; you are not setting your mind on God's interest, but man's."
—Matthew 16:23

Managing our depression can take many forms. That's why there are so many tools in the toolbox. Sometimes one tool works, and sometimes another one does.

I was in therapy once, and the therapist suggested I find a stuffed animal to talk to. "Sit it in a chair and tell it off," she said.

Well, it seemed to me a cute little stuffed animal was just not going to do the trick. It so happened my son had an old, ugly stuffed animal (yes, there are such things) that he was no longer interested in. Do you remember the Tasmanian Devil? It was a TV cartoon and the perfect choice.

I would put it in a chair and tell it off when I needed to. Thank goodness no one heard me. You can do this too. The therapist knew what she was talking about. Here's why it helps.

Depression begins to take on a life of its own. It's almost as if you've lost control of yourself, and depression is now a real entity living inside of you and calling the shots. It's telling you to stay in bed. It's telling you to feel sorry for yourself. It's telling you that you can use it as an excuse to avoid responsibility. It's telling you to watch too much TV or eat too many cookies. After all, you're depressed and sad, so you deserve it. Do you see how convincing that voice can be?

So, if you can begin to see depression as not who you really are, you will start to exercise more control. As long as we feel depression is who we truly are, we will never get better. We don't ask to be depressed. Our own choices may have helped to get us there, and we certainly will need to change some things to keep future episodes at bay, but what's important is to get better first.

Put it in a chair and direct all your frustration and anger at it. Learn to think of your depression as separate from you because when you do, you feel like it's something you can fight. This is not to suggest that self-reflection isn't necessary, but sometimes it just feels good to yell at something.

Remember, depression isn't who you are. It's an illness you are struggling with just like any other illness, despite what anyone else might tell you. It deserves no less an effort to get better either.

It's a process, and some days you will feel you've taken a step backward, but try not to get discouraged when this happens. Even after surgery, there are good days and bad days. If this is a bad day, just take the day off.

Yelling at a stuffed animal won't be for everyone because you might feel silly. You might want to consider just pulling up a chair and pretend depression is sitting there. Be creative in your approach.

Managing depression can be tricky, and what works one day may not work the next. Use these tools however they work the best for you.

Have you ever found yourself angry about your depression? Can you put depression in its place?

DAY 11

DEPRESSION AND ILLNESS

"Be gracious to me, O LORD, for I am in distress."
—Psalm 31:9

Depression's voice is even louder when we are struggling with illness or pain. Pain can be a real catalyst when it comes to our moods. At times, it's hard to decide which is worse, the physical or the mental/emotional. I've been both places at the same time. I haven't decided yet.

The entire time I've been putting the final touches on this book, I've dealt with an undiagnosed intestinal illness. It's been hard at times because I've been out of commission for a few days every week. Losing precious time makes me anxious.

"Why now, Lord?"

Depression is certainly complicated by illness. Strangely though, when we are ill or in pain, we sometimes concentrate on our illness and forget about our depression! So, there's that.

Mild depression can often follow a viral infection. It can also be the temporary side effect of some medications. It's important to know if any of the medications you regularly take could cause depression, which is why I always suggest seeing your doctor to discuss these issues.

When we feel sick enough that we don't want to do anything, but not sick enough to stay in bed, those times can be an invitation for our mood to plummet. I learned to head it off by making myself presentable, keeping the house neat, and so on. Again, it's simple distractions that seem to work so well at times. More about this in the tools section.

Pay attention to your vulnerabilities, particularly your health, and if you have chronic health conditions that flare up, prepare to meet them head-on, and have a plan should your moods plummet. Know how depression works in your life. Don't be caught off guard by a medical illness.

Even as I write today, I am dealing with a reoccurrence of the intestinal issues. I'm taking it easy and cancelling what I need to so I can finish the editing of this book. I made a plan early on that when this flared up, I would stay focused on this book at the cost of pretty much everything else.

I know it's temporary. Sometimes God expects us to sequester ourselves for a period of time when He has a mission for us to fulfill. Can you see how having a plan can be helpful?

I've had five surgeries on my feet. During the recovery periods, one of which was almost a year, I really had to work hard to stay mentally healthy. I love to walk outside or on my treadmill and have found that to be my go-to when dealing with anxiety, so even the thought of more foot surgery puts me in a tailspin. But once again, I have a plan for how to handle inertia so that depression does not rear its ugly head.

King David eloquently recounts this in Psalm 38 where he states in verse 3 that "even his bones ache." Read the whole psalm for a better understanding of the connection he outlines between his mood and his body symptoms.

Illness and pain are a real playground for depression.

Mind-set and determination are powerful deterrents to depression's tentacles. Illness of any kind can send us spiraling if we don't have a plan to deal with it. Easier said than done, but I've done it, so I know it's possible.

Have you found that illness or physical pain makes your depression worse?

Can you develop a plan for future episodes?

DAY 12
WHAT YOU DON'T MONITOR YOU CAN'T CHANGE

> Let us test and examine our way, and return to the LORD.
> —Lamentations 3:40

I'm a real believer in monitoring my life, my actions, my habits, my words, and my thoughts. I used to do this only mentally but quickly learned I have a tendency to overlook a lot.

Socrates said, "The unexamined life is not worth living." I agree with that wholeheartedly, although I would add that self-examination needs to be under God's umbrella. And there are many verses in scripture that support this as well. Read 2 Corinthians 13:5 and Lamentations 3:40.

According to these scriptures, God certainly supports self-examination. The trick, though, is how to think about it, how to do it, and how to implement the results.

First, how to think about it. You must be convinced that monitoring your habits and routines is the only way you will know for sure if you're making progress. It seems like adding a task like journaling when one is already feeling overwhelmed is too much to suggest. I didn't do it for years either. When I did, it was stop and start because I never really knew what I should be monitoring.

Here's a list of some things I track now: health, sleep, exercise, my words and thoughts, Bible study, prayer, blogging, and writing. I don't beat myself if I mess up in one these areas, because there was usually a very good reason. But then I ask, "Is a very good reason an excuse though?" Tracking these items keeps me honest.

Until you fully embrace and understand the importance of monitoring how you are doing, you will always be relying on your memory, and your memory (mine too) is notoriously inaccurate.

Here's a good example.

My mother would often get *sick*, her term for depression. I would track how long she was sick. When she would tell me it had been months, I was able to tell her, "No, Mom, it's been three weeks." And here's where most of us will make the mistake. Because we are down, anxious, or depressed, we have a tendency to think we've had fewer good days than we've really had.

Conversely, we also think we've had more bad days than we really have. Unless we can actually see our progress, our memory will give us a false and discouraging picture.

The how. I use the Bullet method of journaling (BUJO). It's a specific journaling method but can be designed however you want. Some creative types make their journals a work of art. My BUJO is a creative mess. I just want to see at a glance how I'm doing, so that's not important to me.

I used two facing pages. I put the calendar days across the top and the things I'm tracking along the side. I fill in the blanks for successful days and leave the others open. I can look at these pages and know exactly how I'm doing. It's that simple and will probably prove therapeutic.

I also have a daily page for each day of the month to record the day's events, allowing two lines at the most. I jot down notes. It's very brief. Just writing it down encourages me greatly.

What to do with your results. Look at it daily if you can. Look for some patterns. For me, the visual is great. On days your depression was worse, what was going on? Check your daily pages to compare.

    I cannot encourage you enough to do this. Right now, I am closely tracking the words I speak out loud. I'm trying to eliminate harsh and unkind-sounding words in my vocabulary and finding a different way to express my thoughts. It's working.

    I know this is a lot to ask, but I can guarantee it's the only way you will know how you're doing. A word of caution though. If you don't see progress, don't get discouraged. It might simply mean you aren't tracking things accurately, you are tracking too much, or you are being too hard on yourself.

> Are you relying on your memory to know how you're doing? Can you see where having written records could help?

DAY 13

GOD IS WITH YOU ON THIS JOURNEY

> Forgetting what lies behind and reaching
> forward to what lies ahead, I press on.
> —Philippians 3:13–14

That is probably my favorite verse in all of the Bible. It was my mantra for recovery.

This journey to mental health we are on isn't about the *what* or the big *why*. It's about *who*. God will not abandon you as you confront the part you may have played in either causing your depression or exacerbating it. I'm well aware that circumstances and relationships can be a big factor, but just as in every other area in our lives, we play a part as well. But God is with you in this journey regardless of how you fell into the pit.

The apostle Paul was very discouraged at times. From my reading of the Pauline epistles, I would say he probably even dealt with real depression. I base that on the words he wrote about his discouragement. We know that Paul had a history he wasn't proud of. But because he was a new person in Christ, he chose to press on and forget about his past.

Pressing on doesn't mean we have to feel strong first. We seldom have to press on when we feel strong anyway. There's no pressing to be done. It's when we feel weak and fearful that pressing comes into play.

I decided to look up the word *press* in the Strong's concordance.

It links the word closely to pursue. But Strong's also referred me to another Greek word that is similar in spelling. That Greek word is *deilos*, which means timid or fearful. So, my earlier definition is right on target. We press on while we are afraid. We don't wait until we feel strong.

I envision pressing on as something we start from an immobile state. We're stuck. It's like we can barely pick up our feet, like we are wearing concrete shoes. It is with great effort that we take that first step. I believe that is exactly the message Paul is teaching as he refuses to let his past determine his future any longer.

There is a hill by our cabin that seems to go on forever. When it's hot and humid, I find myself pressing on. I know that every deliberate step I take gets me closer to the top. Sometimes I look at the ground instead of looking ahead just so I won't know how far I have yet to go. It would do me no good to turn back the way I came because I already walked down a few hills, so it would mean walking back up those hills to get back to the cabin. There is no way I'm going back and encountering those same hills again, so I press forward and tackle the hill I'm on.

Don't look back at yesterday's hills, especially if they were more like mountains. Don't say, "I just can't do this another day. I can't keep pressing on."

Yes.

You.

Can.

All you must do is keep on keeping on *today*. The next minute. The next five. The next hour.

The things that really matter in life require time and effort.

Our lives and our journeys are different, to be sure. But God walks with us no matter what ground is under our feet. He walks with us on smooth ground or almost impassable ground. He helps us maintain balance when we start to stumble on rocks of despair. He keeps us from slipping when the rocks are wet with our tears.

"He lifted me out of the slimy pit, out of the mud and mire:

He set my feet on a rock and gave me a firm place to stand" (Psalm 40:2).

Regaining our mental health is a rocky road, but God walks with us. Our journey out of depression is made easier when we have His hand to hold on to.

Whose hand are you holding right now?

Can you picture your favorite path and visualize God walking with you?

DAY 14
WHEN DEPRESSION HAS YOU FACEDOWN

> There was a woman who had a spirit of infirmity eighteen years and was bowed together and could not lift herself up. And when Jesus saw her ...
> —Luke 13:10–13

Notice the verse states the woman "could not" lift herself up.

So often, we treat depression as if the sufferer could say the magic words and they'd be healed. "Think positive thoughts," some say. "Just have more faith," others chide. "Read your Bible more. Pray more," these armchair doctors arrogantly state.

When you're on this roller-coaster ride of depression, first you have to get off the ride if your head is going to be clear enough to think. Have you ever tried to make a big decision when you have a bad headache? You simply can't. You wait till it subsides. It's that kind of a thing.

First of all, depression (real depression, not just a few bad days due to an obvious cause) doesn't happen overnight, although it can certainly feel that way. It is usually the culmination of faulty thinking, unhealthy habits, unhealthy behaviors, and continual stress. So yes, in that sense, the ideas suggested by those armchair doctors have some value.

Besides, who doesn't need to have more faith, read their Bible more, and pray more? I think that is probably true of all us if we would be so honest as to admit it. It certainly isn't a prescription unique to depressed people only.

But no matter what the cause, once depression sets up camp in our psyche, it never helps to be told that a quick fix is all it takes to get better. Just do *this* or *that*.

But everyone is a physician when it comes to depression.

The truth is there are a lot of "this's" and "that's" that do help but only when a person is on the road to recovery, not while in the pit. Patients aren't discharged from a hospital, even for outpatient surgery, as soon as the surgery is done. There is always some recovery period, and generally, they have to be able to take a few steps first before they can be released. Why should depression be any different?

This woman described in Luke had suffered eighteen years. I can't imagine. This woman was quite literally bent over and could only see the ground. Consequently, she was often overlooked or nearly stumbled over. While the story doesn't say she suffered depression, I'm thinking she well could have. Who wouldn't when all you've seen for eighteen years is dirt!

I once knew a very sincere Christian woman who suffered with severe anxiety for more than sixty years before she sought help. That's a long time to be bent over. Her spiritual pride got in the way.

We know the woman in this story had a heart that was right with God (there is no sin mentioned), because the first thing she did after her healing was to offer Jesus praise.

Jesus saw her. Let me repeat, Jesus saw her. "When Jesus saw her, he called her over and said, "Woman, you are freed from your illness" (Luke 13:12).

Jesus sees *you* as well.

Jesus didn't say to the woman, "Your sins are forgiven," because there was no specific illness-causing sin to be forgiven.

Sin is not automatically the root or only cause of depression, although it may play a role.

Don't ever judge someone's faith by their depression *or* the lack of it. One doesn't make you a weak Christian, and the other doesn't make you a strong one.

We are all bent over in some way or another.

Have you ever felt completely bent over?
Can you believe that Jesus sees you as well?

DAY 15

MORE ON THE WOMAN BENT OVER

> You are loosed from your infirmity.
> —Luke 13:12

Luke 13:11–16 gave us the story of the woman who was so bent over she couldn't stand up straight. We've all seen people like that—people completely bent over from arthritis. Truly, they are always looking at the ground.

But what about the rest of us?

I approach what I'm writing today cautiously. When we're battling a severe depressive episode, there is a natural inclination for us to want to talk to a lot of people about it. That makes sense. We are hurting so much we just hope someone will come up with a solution. And I'm certainly not suggesting we shouldn't talk to anyone, just not everyone.

What I am suggesting, though, is that we are careful with how much we talk about our depression and with whom.

Have you ever been around someone who always has the same complaint, but for the life of you, you can't figure out what they're doing about it other than complaining? They wear out their welcome pretty quickly. You don't want to be one of them. I like this piece of wisdom from Charles Spurgeon:

"Some of God's children complain about their own weakness, mourn about their own impurity and allow their own emotion to govern their decisions. The one and only subject of their thoughts is their own condition."

Of course, depression is an all-encompassing condition. It's hard to think of anything else but how miserable and hopeless you feel. But it won't help to talk about it over and over. That's called rumination, and it's usually very unhealthy.

We can and should talk to a few close friends and certainly seek professional help if we can afford it. But when we share our pain, it should always be with the view of seeking solutions, working through it with someone, listening to their ideas, mulling it over together.

We need understanding people but not enabling people. Enabling people generally only wallow with us; they don't lift us up. We need *ladder* people, those who inspire us to climb higher.

God understands our preoccupation with ourselves when we're depressed. But He wants us to talk to Him about it first and foremost. Don't be afraid to be totally honest about your pain. After all, Jesus was totally honest about His pain in the garden with His father, our father.

God expects us to keep moving toward Him, even if the only thing we can see is the dirt, even if we have to crawl—as long as we are crawling toward Him.

God sees our journey through the dirt. I believe He hates it as much as we do. And I think He's perfectly fine when we cry out about how much we hate how we're feeling. In fact, I believe that it is then when God starts to heal, when we realize we are at the end of what we can tolerate. We want out, and we believe He is the one who provides the strength to do that.

Remember, God sees so much more than you do. He's calling you to look up instead of looking down. He sees your future wholeness while understanding your present brokenness.

Trust Him on your journey to good mental health. He can and will deliver you if you keep taking that next step.

Have you been making your depression worse by constantly talking about it?

Can you make it a point to talk to God first?

DAY 16
ACTING AS IF

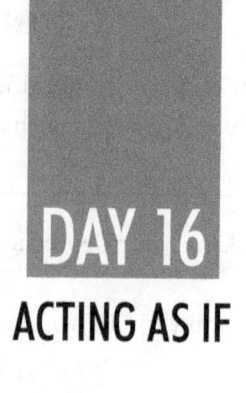

> Be the best imitation of your best self because
> your best self is who you really are.

Have you ever walked into a room of strangers and made yourself look more confident than you are?

Have you ever been in a meeting or at a conference and nodded your head in agreement with what the speaker was saying, but you didn't have a clue?

Well, you already know what *acting as if* is. Only this version is a little different. This type of *faking it until you make it* is all about you and no one else. It's about changing your perception of yourself until your perception of yourself becomes real. It's a type of therapy often suggested by mental health professionals.

The Bible even suggests it. Think about it. Can you think of a single verse that suggests you have to be strong before you attempt anything great for God? In fact, it's just the opposite. Great men and women of God throughout the ages have acted confidently when they were shaking in fear inside. It's when we're the most afraid but keep moving ahead that we are trusting God the most.

That's what this is all about. It means walking, moving, talking, and dressing as though you are not depressed. You are not trying to fool others, but you are trying to fool yourself—your mind anyway. It's back to that mind-body connection.

DEPRESSION HAS A BIG VOICE

Your mind has no idea whether how you're moving, talking, or acting is real or not. But when you are acting as though you are not depressed, when your speech doesn't reflect it, when your body language doesn't suggest it, your brain responds as though this behavior is real. And *you* start to respond as if that's true.

It's not a behavior meant to fool anyone in a deceitful way. It's a behavior you adopt to get yourself out of a slump. It works. For example, when you smile, other people smile back, and it makes you realize the world might not be such a bad place after all. Plus, your smile will probably lift their spirit as well. It's a win-win.

Walking around with our heads down, looking glum, is not going to elicit any positive encounters with people, and positive encounters improve our moods.

If you're wondering if it's possible to smile when you feel really depressed, it is. Trust me, it won't seem genuine at all. That's not the point. The point is to get those signals to your brain. This little movement of turning up the corners of your mouth has been scientifically proven to release good endorphins into your brain, and you will feel a little better. This isn't theory; this is fact.

There is a long section in the original book I wrote that didn't make it into this devotional about how this book came about. Here's the capsulized version.

I was new to our church. I had been a leader in all the other churches, but we had moved. I had never been an attendee in a Bible study because I always led them. A study was beginning at our new church, and my husband insisted I go for at least one night.

I lingered in the hallway for a long time. I didn't want to go in because I felt like such an outsider. I knew my husband would be disappointed, so for him only, I found a seat. Wouldn't you know, I had lingered too long and was stuck at a front table. No one knew how anxious I felt because I knew about this little technique and had used it in my life to overcome all-consuming anxiety.

That night, God spoke through our leader and through the woman who was teaching in the video. (In case you are wondering, it was a Beth Moore video.) What was said that night by Ms. Moore, our leader, and the women at the table confirmed I was hearing correctly, "Write a book."

Had I not acted as if and walked confidently into that room, I probably wouldn't have heard this call. No one is as confident as they seem anyway. Everyone has, at one time or another, had to do this.

Can you see how this works?

Will you try today to act like the nondepressed person you want to be?

DAY 17

FAITH AND TRUST: THE DIFFERENCE

> There is all the difference in the world between a man's status and position on the one hand, and his experience on the other.
> —L. Martin Lloyd-Jones

I woke up in the middle of the night wondering about the difference between faith and trust. Was there one? I already had my sixty days, so that meant a page would have to be replaced.

Aren't you wondering what was here before? It was a lot of statistics you probably wouldn't have been interested in anyway. And it all boiled down to the fact that depression is an equal-opportunity employer. It can be experienced by anyone at any time, no matter their age, finances, or education; none of it makes a difference to depression. That was basically it. And, oh, women are twice as likely to suffer depression because of the whole hormonal gyrations. So, there you have it.

Anyway, I came to the conclusion that faith and trust are two different things. From my study, I concluded we can have faith in God and faith in His Word and yet not *trust* Him with our day-to-day lives. We prescribe to faith, we say we have faith, but for many, that's where it ends. We haven't learned to trust. And if we're suffering from depression, in particular, it's very hard to trust.

Here are some practical examples from some giants of faith:

Abraham had faith, but he *trusted* when he took his only son up a hill to be sacrificed.

Moses had faith, but he *trusted* when he confronted Pharaoh.

David had faith, but he *trusted* when he went out to fight Goliath.

So, how does trust work with depression?

Trust means we trust God about all the aspects of depression we are struggling with. Trust means we let Him know we're having a really bad day, and then we believe He is in the process of healing. Trust means our faith is in a person, not just a system of beliefs.

We trust a person, not a concept. We trust God.

I used to question my faith, the amount I had anyway. It seemed I had so little compared to those I listened to or read about. I confused faith with trust. I thought faith meant I would feel a certain way. I thought my words would sound more, well, holy. I didn't think I sounded like I really was a believer when I spoke. I would chastise myself at times over what I felt was my inadequacy.

Then I realized I was coming to God first about pretty much everything in my life. Nothing was too small, too big, too confusing, too scary, or too anything. Wait a minute. Now, I *was* confused. Were they two different things, or at the very least, did one spring from the other? I reconsidered how I had been thinking about faith.

That was faith! I do have faith. *Trusting God for all the particulars in our lives is faith.*

Suddenly, my little grain of mustard seed started growing into a plant. I still wish I had more, but I've come to the conclusion that only God can decide if I have enough or not. All I have to do is trust. Faith comes by hearing the Word of God, so the more I study His Word, the more my faith will come anyway (Romans 10:17).

With depression, it's particularly important not to get caught up in questioning the strength or the amount of your faith, because then you will start to doubt you will be healed if you feel your faith is not strong enough.

Trust that God is with you and He is not judging the amount of faith you have, because if you are trusting Him, you have faith. Even a mustard seed is enough.

Are you questioning your faith?
Can you focus on trust instead?

DAY 18
HOW DEPRESSION STEALS OUR TIME

> Yet you do not know what tomorrow will bring.
> What is your life? For you are as a mist that
> appears for a little time and then vanishes.
> —James 4:14

Depression is a master robber.

It robs our time

Every time we allow depression to steal even one minute, sixty fleeting seconds, that's time we will never get back. We don't know what tomorrow brings. We don't know how much time we have left. That's not morbid. It's just true. So, why let depression eat up even one more day?

It's been said countless times that we have only this moment. When you're depressed, however, that's almost a welcome thought, because the thought of any more minutes feeling like you do is unthinkable. But you can change that for your future by taking away depression's influence on your today.

I wish I had realized years ago just what a time robber depression is; I just never equated the two. But it's so true.

Not only does it rob of us the present time; it robs us of future time as well. That's because the time we waste today has removed certain choices we might have tomorrow, or at least made them harder. If I'm a slug today, then tomorrow I will probably have to play catch-up. It becomes a constant catch-up, and I never do what I really want to. I'm always a day behind.

Depression robs us of moments we don't even know we could have had. It robs us of our dreams. Of all the damage depression does, stealing our time is one of the most destructive. Yes, we can continue to dream no matter how many days depression has stolen, but let's face it, some dreams need time, precious time, to accomplish. And every minute depression steals is time taken away from fulfilling those dreams. I know.

Depression has a life of its own. Every day you choose to let depression gobble up your time is a choice that was made for you, not by you. It was made by the enemy.

Every time depression calls the shots, you are the one paying. Every minute depression steals only hurts you. Satan loves it when he steals your time because he knows he's ultimately stealing your life.

And when depression can steal your time from God, Satan is particularly gleeful. Nothing pleases him more than to see a Christian ignoring their maker. Satan is the happiest when we feel the most distant from God.

Satan knows the more time he can steal by keeping us depressed, the more repair work will have to be done to get back on track. He knows the more he can eat up our time, the less time we will give to God.

In other words, depression fills up your tomorrows with struggles that could have been avoided by making different time choices today.

Do you see where this is heading?

Make a decision today to get better. Make a decision today to make the cost-ratio benefit more benefit and less cost. It starts with a decision. Everything does.

Aren't you tired of paying such a high cost for an illness that is robbing you of so much? It makes no sense, does it?

How has depression robbed you of time?
Would you like to be sure it doesn't take anymore?

DAY 19
GRACE AND MEDICATION

> My grace is sufficient for you.
> —2 Corinthian's 12:9

I have mixed feelings about medication. I have been on antidepressants in the past. They helped in the initial phase, but they certainly didn't banish it.

Sometimes medication gets in the way of progress because once we start feeling better, we forget how bad we *used* to feel. It all becomes a distant memory, so we don't feel the need to work on anything. We're feeling better, and that's all that matters to us.

I guess that makes some sense. There are those who simply don't want to wait. And despite what the ads say about it taking six weeks before you notice a difference, everyone I know has experienced a little relief in the first few weeks. That's just enough to get them to that six-week mark when most of the medication's effects will have kicked in.

But with medication comes side effects, plenty of them. For some, the initial side effects are too difficult to adjust to, and people quit taking it. Then the depression returns full force. It's a tough call sometimes, and only you and your doctor can decide which is best for you.

So, we could ask, is it grace or medication we need?

We certainly need the grace but medication may well be the means by which we find it. We might need both.

I'm sure of one thing. If depression is robbing us of our lives, and if medication is suggested, by all means take it. It would be wrong not to. There is no honor in suffering when you don't have to.

God may choose to send grace in the form of a pill. As far as I know, God's grace is not limited to only those ways we would label spiritual. God's grace can show up any way He can, because like God, grace is unfathomable and unlimited.

Here's the thing though. We can't borrow grace from the future to handle our present struggles. We can't store it up for a rainy day either. And most importantly, grace is more than a feeling. Grace is a state of being. It is the by-product of divine influence upon our hearts. It means all is well with our soul.

Grace is undeserved.

Grace is free.

Grace does not discriminate.

Grace, most importantly, *does not depend on anything we do.* God is the author of grace, and only God gets to decide how and when He dispenses it.

So, how do you know when you are receiving grace? When I wrote that question, I immediately asked myself, "How do *I* know?"

The word *grace* is used in a few different ways in the scriptures. I settled on 2 Corinthians 12:9 for our discussion. "My grace is sufficient for you."

Grace, not strength, is what empowers us. We might not feel strong, but God says we are at our most powerful when we feel our weakest. It is at our weakest that God's grace is the most sufficient.

When we really *get*—as in understand—grace, when we embrace it, we become like children being held by a loving father. It's good to feel God's arms around us. We feel secure. We sense that well-being. It's that sense of knowing God's got this. We feel safe.

For those of you who didn't have that with your earthly father, you can have that now with your heavenly one.

How often do you experience grace?
Do you believe that grace is for you?

DAY 20
DON'T COMPARE AND THEN DESPAIR

> I will give thanks to you, for I am
> fearfully and wonderfully made.
> —Psalm 139:14

People with low self-esteem are very prone to depression. And people with low-esteem often feel that way because they negatively compare themselves with others.

What is it about comparisons that make our moods plummet? Without a doubt, it's our personal lack of self-esteem. If we really felt good about ourselves in the first place, comparisons wouldn't be problematic for us. At the same time, we tell ourselves that if we feel good about ourselves, we are narcissistic. We chastise ourselves with, "Shouldn't I be more concerned with how God esteems me than how I esteem myself?"

And, of course, we should. But that doesn't mean we should hang our heads in false humility either. Besides, no one likes to be negatively compared to someone else. I've been there myself on more than one occasion, and I came home whimpering like a hurt animal. But guess what?

We do it to ourselves all the time. It doesn't have to come from outside us because it's already in us, just waiting for someone to tap into our vulnerability.

We see someone dressed exactly right, and we look at what

we're wearing and think, *I'm such a slob.* I had a little victory with this the other day. I saw a young woman at a clothing store. She was beautiful. The great thing though? She didn't act like it. You could just tell.

She was trying on a pair of pants and came out of the dressing room to show her mother. Seeing as I was right there, I remarked at how great they looked on her. Of course, she was years younger, so it was easy. But it took the sting out of that whole comparison thing for a few minutes.

But wouldn't you know it, that same day (was God trying to teach me a lesson or what?), I was in another store (I really don't shop that much) and encountered a woman much closer to my age. She was stunning, from her perfect hair and makeup down to her perfect shoes. I immediately looked at myself in my jeans and aerobic shoes and thought, *What a mess. Why didn't I at least change shoes?* I quickly headed down a different aisle. I was so embarrassed.

We are invited over to someone's house for dinner, and they cook an outstanding meal, and immediately we come to the conclusion that we are lousy cooks. Someone else golfs better or is more successful in their job. Someone else's house is beautifully decorated, and our mood drops. Someone else is smarter, more talented—it goes on and on, doesn't it?

There will always be someone who is "er" than us and "iest" than us. It's the "ers" and "iests" that get us every time. In case I need to explain, "er" is smarter, cuter, and so on, while "iest" is smartest, prettiest, and whatever else you can think of.

Sometimes we even go so far as to distance ourselves from people we feel are somehow more than us. That's not fair to them, and it's certainly not good for us because we can't always avoid these people anyway.

The ironic part is that while you're comparing yourself to someone else, someone else is comparing themselves to you, and you are the *more than*. That pendulum comparison swings both ways. But we never think about that, do we?

So, what do we do? I think there is only one solution.

We remember whose we are and what we are. We are children of the King, and we are royalty. We are loved for who we are. God never compares us to anyone. I just love that.

I want you to try something the next time you look in the mirror, especially if you're having a bad hair day. When you're looking at yourself and not liking what you see, imagine God standing behind you looking in that same mirror.

He sees you as well, but He says, "You are fearfully and wonderfully made" (Psalm 139:14). Translated, "You are beautiful."

Remember, God sees a beautiful creation when He sees *you*. He thinks *you* are beautiful.

Do you find yourself comparing yourself to others?
Does your mood drop when you do?

DAY 21
OUR TRIGGERS ARE UNIQUE

> We are what we habitually do.
> —Aristotle.

What causes your mood to suddenly drop? We already mentioned comparisons. But there are other causes.

Do you find that you're having a perfectly wonderful day, and then someone says something and your mood plummets? Or you read a Facebook post and find that in a few hours, you are feeling down? What happened is that something triggered your mood to drop.

Triggers are an important topic in the subject of depression, and not all triggers are the same. Have you thought much about your triggers? Or does it seem the bottom falls out of your mood, and you are shaking your head wondering what brought it on? That's very normal until you begin to know your areas of vulnerability.

Mine are primarily fatigue, feeling overwhelmed, clutter, and poor sleep. If I don't sleep well, I am tired and thus easily overwhelmed. And I particularly feel overwhelmed if I'm surrounded by too much clutter. There is a direct link between clutter and our moods. For many people, clutter is draining and overwhelming. Clutter needs to kept under control so your moods can be as well.

Only you can decide what excess clutter looks like for you, but don't deceive yourself. Piles of stuff lying around with no home is clutter, and clutter drains our energy, especially when we are depressed. It is physically exhausting. There are many websites that offer ways to manage your clutter. I absolutely can't write if there is a bunch of stuff lying in my field of vision, and I'm not compulsively neat by any stretch of the imagination.

Fatigue is a common trigger. The problem isn't the fatigue so much as the effects of the fatigue.

We all have different triggers, and it's important to identify them and then find ways to mitigate them. I would love to know what your triggers are. (faighsighaddiy.com/underhiswings)

We feel overwhelmed and anxious when we are overly tired. Our thinking becomes foggy. We walk around dazed. The problem is that the fatigue messes with our minds, resulting in foggy thinking. Poor sleep, fatigue, and feeling overwhelmed are closely related. Does any of this sound familiar to you?

People and circumstances can be triggers as well. For example, someone in your household who is very negative can affect your mood. An employer who is constantly berating you can affect you as well. It could be a spouse or a parent. But that doesn't mean it has to result in clinical depression.

Again, it's a matter of knowing yourself, knowing how to respond to certain people and life events and then having a plan when confronted with these issues.

We have to work hard to recognize our triggers by paying attention to our moods. When they drop, we should immediately look back over the prior few days and try to determine what events might have triggered our mood drop. (This is where tracking your moods becomes so important.) Often, we will realize how we've allowed disturbing events to build up over time, and the result was snowballing into a real downer.

Start thinking back to when you felt your mood dropping. Engage in some reflection. (No morbid introspection, however.)

There may be times you can't find the cause. That's OK as long as you realize there probably were some precipitating factors.

Some of those factors may have been in your control, and some may not have been. Your reaction to them is what matters.

Remember, depression tries to tell you that you have no control over your responses to your life.

Depression lies.

Have you ever thought about triggers before?
Do you see why knowing your triggers could help?

DAY 22
WHEN YOU JUST WANT TO BE LEFT ALONE

> Many are the plans in a man's heart, but it is
> the LORD'S purpose that prevails.
> —Proverbs 19:21 (NIV)

Living depression-free would be easier if we didn't have to deal with people. Right?

Interject the drama and demands of others, and our faith walk can get a little bogged down. Add depression to the mix—and whoa, it gets complicated.

But God's plan has always been for companionship. He created Eve so Adam wouldn't be alone. He doesn't intend for us to live our lives without meaningful relationships either. But how in the world do we do that when we're struggling to just get out of bed? The answer is both simple and difficult.

We try to think of someone other than ourselves.

We force ourselves to make that phone call to a friend. We literally slap ourselves up alongside the head, and with every ounce of strength we have, we reach out to someone else. We purposefully look for a need and try to fill it. If there is nothing else we can do, we make sure we are praying for others. Intercessory prayer certainly isn't a "nothing else," but sometimes it's all we can muster.

Even though we are feeing unloved, isolated, lonely, and generally miserable, here's the thing: there is always someone much worse off than we are. Hard to believe, but it's true.

"But how do we do this?" you ask. "I just can't. I just don't have it in me right now," you say to yourself.

Well, if you have breath, you *are* quite capable of doing this.

I know because I learned to do it, and I've been as depressed as anyone. I learned I functioned better when I connected with people, even if they didn't know how bad I was feeling. Just being with others, even if you don't know them, can have a mood-lifting effect.

We are not meant to fight this battle alone. We need trusted friends we can call on a really hard day and just say, "I'm having a hard time today. Can we just talk for a while?"

There are times being alone is good, but if you're depressed, you're probably doing too much of that anyway. I personally like a day or two of solitude, but I'm careful not to let it become a habit. Now that I am depression-free, I go only a few days before I reach out to others. And while texting isn't ideal, it's still a connection.

I can remember having some bad days, not a full-out case of depression, just being down in the dumps. I thought I needed some me time. I even prayed for that, thinking God would agree with me. But in the course of those few days, I was so inundated with people and their issues I had absolutely no time to myself. God always knows what is best for us, and when I looked back, I realized people, not isolation, was God's plan.

Withdrawing from people is one of the most common symptoms of depression, yet it's often counterproductive. We don't even have to tell anyone how we're feeling. Just exchanging pleasantries can be beneficial. A casual conversation about nothing important can be therapeutic.

Engaging with people when we are depressed is one of the hardest things to do, yet it is one of the most helpful. There will be times when being alone is exactly what you need, but it might prove more beneficial when you are doing better.

Remember, you don't have to pretend anything. Tell God you don't want to be around anyone. You don't want to talk to anyone. You just want to be left alone.

I dare you. I double-dog-dare you.

When you're depressed, do you want to just be left alone? Can you say it really helps?

DAY 23

WHEN IT'S JUST TOO MUCH

> And being in agony He was praying fervently.
> —Luke 22:44

I woke up one night wondering if I should include this page or not. After all, this was not something I wanted family and friends to read. But because it's so far in the past, I decided I would. I knew if a reader was suffering from clinical depression and in a very dark place, when they read this, at the very least, it would let them know they are not alone.

I am referring to the overwhelming sense of dread, the elephant sitting on your chest that actually brings you to the point of wanting to give up. You can't imagine what it would be like to deal with this misery a moment longer. It's been a long struggle already, and enough is enough.

I can remember one particular day many years ago when the depression was so heavy I didn't feel like I could continue the fight. I just wanted the pain to go away. I was in a very scary place. God felt distant, and I so needed to feel His nearness. I had prayed and prayed for the pain to go away.

I had been regular in my devotional time. I was even teaching Bible classes. I had been suffering from depression for a number of years at the time. My doctor had added a medication to help with the increasing anxiety, but it made the anxiety even worse.

It felt as dark as this bar below. No end in sight, as black as it could be.

I didn't know what to do. I started pacing. I kept moving, and as I did, I would see something that needed straightening, something that needed a home, and it would distract me. I just kept walking around and puttering with no plan. It was as if I knew that I had to keep moving. After a few hours, I realized I was feeling a little less overwhelmed. It was still dark, but a lighter dark, like the bar below.

I would like to say I got to this next color right away, but I didn't. But it was enough so I could at least breathe.

I had a lot of work to do after that, but it was the first time I realized that just the act of physical movement could make a difference. I quit the second medication immediately. I started reading and researching and paying attention to simple things that brought relief, and I started to get better.

Now, you may be wondering, why didn't the praying work? But it did, didn't it?

God was wanting to heal me right along, but not without my cooperation. I find scripture is filled with examples of individuals who requested healing from God, yet there was more they were required to do either before or after the healing. Of course, God has healed those who haven't even asked. That's His prerogative. He could have healed me that day.

But this book would not have been written if He had. I wouldn't have been able to share my struggles with hundreds through speaking engagements, workshops, Bible studies, retreats, and my blog. God's timing was perfect.

When we realize that we can't just expect God to do it all while we sit around like a lump, our recovery begins. As I said, I share this with you because if you ever get to this place, reach out to someone. Don't suffer in silence. Call someone immediately. While my experience turned out OK, toughing it out wasn't necessarily the best way to go.

The darkness we can feel at times, while overpowering, is transient. We can find our way out. Depression can be overcome.

Are you feeling overwhelmed today by it all?
Can you—no, will you—call out to God for relief?

DAY 24

SPIRITUAL DEPRESSION

> Why are you downcast, O, My soul?
> —Psalm 43:5

Many Christians confuse their depression with their spirituality. Let me explain.

Christians who feel depressed often jump to the conclusion that it is their spiritual health, or the lack of it to be more precise, that is the issue. They haven't prayed enough. They haven't done enough Bible study. They haven't been involved enough in church ministry. And so it goes as Satan heaps on the guilt.

Or they think they've done something wrong. They look for all kinds of reasons. Instead of accepting the fact that they are human just like everyone else, they cling to the idea they should be above experiencing depression. They conclude it's their spirituality. Of course, there is such a thing as a spiritual depression. Here is my definition of what I would call a spiritual depression:

A spiritual depression is the result of continual practice of known sin or some kind of disobedience.

So, the first question to ask is, "Is there known sin in my life that I simply will not give up?" I don't think any of us are really blind about this. We pretend not to know, but we know.

Until those sins are acknowledged, confessed, and renounced (evidenced by change), our depression will probably continue.

Secondly, has God called you to do something and you are balking? That, too, can lead to a spiritual depression. Spend time with God, however much you need, and seek clarification. What is God asking you to do that perhaps you have turned a blind eye and a deaf ear to?

But spiritual issues are not usually the cause for most Christians' depression. In fact, I would dare say Satan would love for Christians to think their depression is because they are out of step with God. Satan loves it when we feel we are spiritually unhealthy. What a nice breeding ground for him to work.

Satan is a master manipulator and the father of all lies.

Depression causes us to doubt our relationship with God. We feel distant. We feel He is not listening. We feel abandoned at times. This is normal. It's harder to pray when we are seriously depressed; it's harder to read our Bibles. But that doesn't mean it's because our spiritual lives are a mess. It means we are ill.

Feeling guilty because we think we've missed the mark spiritually only adds to our despair. And if there is real guilt because of sin or disobedience, Christ says to confess it to Him, and we are forgiven. There may be consequences, but we will be on our road to a new beginning.

If you're really unsure as to whether your depression is spiritual or not, ask God to reveal those areas that need to come under scrutiny. I can tell you this. During my most severe depressive episode, there was nothing in my life that would qualify my depression as *only* spiritual.

Depression, because of the nature of the illness, causes us to question all of our relationships. As Christians, because our relationship with God is the most important, we question that one the most. As long as we do, we will feel distant from God.

Remember, no matter how you feel, this is the time to reach out to your heavenly Father. He is not abandoning you. He has not moved one iota. He is waiting to cover you with His wings so you can find refuge.

Do not let your feelings run rampant. If you know there is no known sin or disobedience, it means your depression has come from somewhere else. Keep praying. Keep reading. Keep reaching out. Satan would love for you to believe your depression is the result of a spiritual problem.

Don't let Satan win this battle. And certainly don't let your depression turn into a spiritual one by allowing these thoughts to fester.

Have you felt at times that your depression is because you have failed as a Christian?

Can you see how Satan would like you to feel like that way?

DAY 25
KEEP GOD IN THE EQUATION

> The LORD is the one who goes ahead of you;
> he will be with you he will not fail you or
> forsake you. Do not fear or be dismayed.
> —Deuteronomy 31:8

So often, mood disorders complicate our spirituality as well as our depression. We feel guilty about feeling depressed, so we become slack in our spiritual disciplines. Our mood deepens further as we feel more and more distanced from God. We lose track of what caused what. Did our distancing cause the mood drop, or did our mood drop cause the distancing? After a while, it doesn't matter anyway.

We look to the future and see only the unknown. We might see the path, but we don't see Him *on* the path. We simply leave God out of the equation. And that's where a lot of our trouble really starts. We recall God's faithfulness to us in many past situations. We can see His faithfulness in our present situation, but somehow, we just cannot project that same faithfulness to future situations.

But unless we can find a way to do that, we will always be seeing the woods but not the path through the woods.

Don't look to the future without remembering that God is in your future just as He is with you in the present. Keep God in the equation.

"Let not your heart be troubled, trust in me," John 14:1–3, is the command we have to remember when we look to the future, especially if our depression has convinced us we will never get better.

I have one specific fear, which I will keep private, that sparks panic every time I linger on it too long. It's like I almost want to get there so I can get past it. Know what I mean? When we think of that what-if scenario, it's always in the future, isn't it? That's where most fear lies, in the future.

We forget that God is with us now, so we need to deal with it now. If our future fear does happen, God will also be there, right there, in that moment. The *there* will become the now once again, and once again, God will help us in the now.

As stated before, we are never promised a particular grace ahead of when it's necessary. It's kind of like a prescription. We get it when we need it. A doctor doesn't write a prescription for you based on what might happen in the future.

And we won't get someone else's prescription of grace either, only our own.

We all know we shouldn't worry about the future. But worry and depression go hand in hand. While we might be able to handle our worry under normal circumstances, when our mood is really low, our worries intensify. We don't see the hope. We certainly don't feel the hope. We borrow a lot of future trouble when we are depressed.

I did it just today. I am putting the final touches on this book before submitting it. My fear of failure is in full swing this morning. I was as honest in prayer as I have ever been, admitting to God that I was having a hard time trusting Him for the future of this book.

It felt so good to admit it out loud, without reservation or editing, and then to find reassurance from His Word. I felt His arms around me and heard Him whisper, "Just trust."

DEPRESSION HAS A BIG VOICE

Oswald Chambers says in *My Utmost for His Highest*, "All our fret and worry is caused by calculating without God."

Remember, don't calculate the future without God.

Can you admit your greatest fear about the future?

Now, will you take that fear to God and tell Him about it?

DAY 26
WHY FORGIVENESS MATTERS

> Purify me with hyssop, and I shall be clean.
> Wash me, and I shall be whiter than snow.
> —Psalm 51:7

When you harbor resentments and grudges toward others, it is extremely difficult to overcome depression and anxiety. You know how it feels inside when you are angry and resentful. It feels terrible. And the worst part? It doesn't hurt anyone as much as you.

Forgiveness is almost always a process. When you see someone interviewed on TV after a horrific event, and they quickly forgive the perpetrator, their forgiveness is often in words only. Real forgiveness means carefully thinking through what you really mean when you say you forgive.

It is necessary to know why you are forgiving someone and what you are forgiving them for, and it's not quickly done. It's also necessary to determine in advance how you will respond to this person (or people) in the future. As a general rule, forgiveness requires some deep thinking.

Forgiveness is also more than a feeling, and the truth is, your feelings may never catch up. That's OK. But you don't have to feel anger or bitterness either. Remember, forgiveness is not absolution. Only God can completely absolve someone, and when He does, even then there could still be serious consequences.

Forgiveness also doesn't mean you have to reestablish a relationship with the person you are forgiving. An abused woman, for example, does not need to put herself back in harm's way after she has forgiven her husband.

Forgiveness is mercy extended to the offender and to yourself. Mercy says you will no longer let their offense consume you. You free them, and you free yourself.

So why anyone hangs onto bitter, angry feelings is beyond me. It's been said unforgiveness is like drinking poison yourself while expecting the other person to die. It makes no sense.

But I have a hunch there is one person in particular, someone you know well, who needs forgiveness before they can move on. That someone is you. I've never known a person, not one, who suffers from depression who doesn't also have a keenly developed conscious. Overly so, I might add.

People who are arrogant and feel superior to everyone else, people who take advantage of other people, these people almost never get depressed. Why would they? They can always find someone else or some circumstance to blame.

I grew up feeling responsible for my world. I believed that the trauma I experienced as a child was all my fault. I should've been able to fix it. I should've been able to make everyone happy.

I don't know your past. There may be things you have done for which you are legitimately guilty. I've made my own mistakes as well and rightly felt the guilt that went along with my actions.

If you've never brought those past mistakes before God, do it now so you can move on. Can you forgive yourself for those mistakes? And if you've confessed them, why are you still holding on to them? It's OK to let them go.

Moving on from your mistakes doesn't make you shallow. It makes you forgiven.

Yes, you may still have to make some things right. You may have to apologize.

But can you forgive yourself for those things over which you had no responsibility at all? And I'll just best those are the things that are getting in your way to complete recovery. I suggest you read the masterpiece on forgiveness, *Forgive and Forget* by Lewis B. Smedes.

There is no person on this earth who God won't forgive if asked. No one. Including you.

Can you stop right now and ask God to forgive you for things you've done wrong?

Will you forgive yourself?

DAY 27

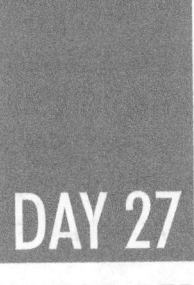

PREPARING FOR DEPRESSION

> He went out, no knowing where he was going.
> —Hebrews 11:8

The winter of 2018 was brutal for most of the country. At one point, our local news station suggested everyone leave their water dripping overnight to prevent water lines from freezing. My husband and I were way ahead of them.

Because our home was built around 1906 (could be older), we need to be a little more aggressive when we have weather like this.

We rolled up fabric and put it on each window ledge. But mostly we worked in the basement, completely covering the windows with carpet tiles. We couldn't believe the difference. The house was much warmer.

And here's the point:

We wanted to wake up the next morning and look forward to a good day. We didn't want to have to deal with broken water lines. We took the steps necessary to ensure we wouldn't wake up to a disaster.

Depression is one of those illnesses where preparedness is really important. That sounds a little strange, but here's what I mean. You need to do those things today that will make you feel better tomorrow. It will give you a sense that you are, in fact, on the road to recovery. And one of those steps is belief.

You have to believe you will get better. That is necessary preparation.

So today, I suggest you speak it out loud to yourself, "I believe I'm going to get better. I believe God is with me on this journey." Say it as often as you need. Prompt yourself with sticky notes like you did with the word *hope* and put it everywhere you think it will help.

I couldn't imagine taking this journey through the dark night of depression without believing that God was walking with me through the valley of despair. "Yea, though I walk through the valley of darkness, you are with me. I will not be afraid because You will comfort me" (Psalm 23:4).

I have no idea where you are in this journey of faith, or whether or not you have even begun. But I know this:

God has only to be invited, and He will walk ahead of you clearing the way, while He also walks beside you in your pain. God does not judge you because you are depressed. He does not love you any less. God understands the emotional and mental pain we go through, which is why so much of what we read in the Bible addresses our depressed moods, our anxiety, and our fears.

Do you think any of that would be addressed in the scriptures were it not for the fact that God knew this would be our experience while on this earth?

Like many, you might not know where you are going on this journey, what is around the corner, what the next day might look like. But like countless others before you, you can step out in faith.

- Don't be afraid to step out in faith and take that first step to get better.
- Don't linger in your depression.
- Don't let it rob you of another moment of your life.
- Don't let it destroy a relationship, cost you a job, or negatively impact your health.

Keep repeating some version of "I believe I am going to get better. God is with me on this journey."

Believe it or not, just saying this today sets you up for success tomorrow.

Are you ready to take this journey to wholeness?
Are you willing to do the necessary work?

DAY 28

LIVING BELOW THE CLOUDS

> Can anyone understand the spreading of the
> clouds, the thundering of His pavilion?
> —Job 36:29

It's not easy maintaining a positive attitude when dark clouds seemed stalled over our heads and there's a lot of stuff going on in our lives. While there is a break in the clouds on occasion, mostly it's overcast. God seems to have spread a gray sheet between Him and us.

Would you agree we all have days like that? Sometimes a number of them in a row. We're not clinically depressed. We don't need medication. We don't need therapy. We just need a break from the unrelenting, cloud-shrouded life.

Sometimes it seems we are continually bombarded with life-depleting events. The furnace breaks down. Someone loses their job. Someone's heart is broken.

When we find when we're under gray clouds, it helps to remember the transient nature of clouds. Even today as I write, the sky overhead can't seem to make up its mind. Will the clouds be given permission to part so the sun/Son can shine through, or will they remain huddled together in a solid mass all day long?

I find I respond in two ways to the dark clouds. If I'm already having a thoughtful and reflecting kind of day, I might actually prefer clouds. If I've planned a day to stay inside and pursue a creative project, I kind of like gray days. Gray days are not always bad. When the clouds match my mood, it makes some sort of convoluted sense.

It's like friends. When we're in the dumps, we usually seek out friends who we know will try to match our moods in their manner of speech and choice of words. We don't need them to act depressed, of course, but we don't want someone who acts too cheerful either; that seems cold and insensitive.

Sometimes a pep talk is needed but not in a "rah, rah" cheerleader fashion. We should try as well to make sure we act appropriately when we're the ones listening. Something I experienced a few years ago brought that home to me.

I was in a meeting at church, and we were discussing poverty. I mentioned how blessed I felt when compared to the rest of the world. One individual (I learned later) misconstrued what I said and felt I was saying I was better than other people because God had blessed me. I wasn't even thinking along those lines. I was just feeling grateful for my life when compared to 90 percent of the world.

I guess it's all how you look at things. Glass half-empty or glass half-full? I wasn't aware that this person was struggling with some serious issues at the time. To someone who wasn't feeling very blessed himself, my remarks must have felt like cold water splashed in his face. While I would say the same thing again—because why wouldn't I say I felt blessed?—I would be careful to explain what I meant.

Now I try to remember that while my clouds have moved for the time being, someone else's clouds may have just shown up. I wished the person in our meeting could have seen my past and the clouds that once hovered over me; he wouldn't have been so quick to judge. That example always stands as a reminder to me not to do the same thing to someone else.

On those days when the clouds aren't welcome, I remind

myself that clouds, by their very nature, eventually move. (Of course, if you live in Michigan as I do, you might have to wait weeks, not days.) Eventually, the sun/Son does break through.

It's just the unrelenting nature of life. Some days we have to look to the heavens and wait for the sky to change, knowing that the Son is only hidden behind the clouds.

What are gray days like for you?
Have you come up with a plan to handle them?

DAY 29

THE WOMAN IN BARNES AND NOBLE

> In as much as you have done it to the least
> of these, you have done it to me.
> —Matthew 25:40

Depression is a self-absorbing illness. Why wouldn't it be? We feel miserable, so we are constantly thinking about our misery. But sometimes God puts another miserable soul in our way, and if we're smart, we will take our eyes off ourselves and notice them.

I was having a bad day, so I headed to our local Barnes and Noble bookstore. It was a wintry day, hubby was out of town, and I didn't want to be alone. At the same time, I didn't want to talk to anyone. I just wanted people around me. Weird, but it works for me.

I found the perfect overstuffed chair away from everyone. I gathered up a pile of books about everything from home decorating to art and, of course, depression. If anyone had looked at that stack of titles, they might have thought I had some serious issues.

I stacked them on the floor, threw my coat on the chair so no one would take my spot (I'm territorial and selfish that way), and picked up the latte I had ordered a few minutes prior. I sat my coffee on the table and flopped into the chair. I was looking forward to hours of reading with no interruptions, except perhaps for more coffee. After a few minutes, I heard some sniffling from the woman seated in the chair next to me at the other side of the table.

Really, Lord? I sighed. *I mean, really?* After a few minutes, *OK, OK, I'll do it!*

There wasn't anyone around, so I leaned over and quietly asked her if I could help. To my surprise (I mean, seriously, why was I surprised? God does this to me often), she opened up and shared her pain with me. I just listened. Eventually, she finished. She got up to leave and said, "Thank you for listening. It really helped."

I told her she was welcome and I would pray for her. It was up to God what happened next. I didn't feel the need to unload on her about faith and God. I felt it was my place to plant a seed. I'm trusting someone else watered her, and God gave someone else the increase (1 Corinthians 3:6).

We are called to do what we are called to do even when we are depressed.

It's interesting how when we are so low, we think we are given a free pass from doing the right thing. Our depression becomes an excuse for avoiding what we just don't feel like doing. However, depression is never an excuse to avoid doing the right thing.

In case you're wondering, no, my depression didn't miraculously go away because of my obedience. It doesn't work that way. But was I able to look back on my day and feel good about it? Yes. And that was a very good thing.

Be on the alert for these encounters, especially when you are feeling rotten. Why? Because every time you encounter a needy soul and you respond, you are reminded that we all have something in common. In a strange way, it loosens the grip depression has on us.

Depression can make us more sensitive to the hurts of others because we have an inner radar. I could've assumed she was sniffling because she had a cold, but as I said, the Holy Spirit was pretty insistent that day, and I've learned to recognize His voice. Plus, I've learned to spot the little signs of depression.

Honestly, did I want to be obedient? I can't say I did. But did that obedience accomplish something I couldn't have known at the time? Yes. That incident turned out to be the perfect story for today.

Never underestimate how helping someone today will positively impact your future tomorrow. And the reverse is also true. Avoiding helping someone, when it's obvious you should, will have a negative impact on your future. While the saying "what goes around comes around" certainly isn't always true, why not believe that it is? It's a good motivator.

Do you agree that we are more sensitive to another person's pain when we're depressed?

Can you be on the lookout for these encounters in the future?

DAY 30

LOWER YOUR EXPECTATIONS

> Do not think of yourself more highly than you ought,
> but rather think of yourself with sober judgment.
> —Romans 12:3 (NIV)

We have an adorable cabin up in northern Michigan. I call it Teeny Tiny Red Cabin. We have added a bedroom so it's not as teeny tiny, but it's still very small, around seven hundred square feet. I also have a she-shed that is over-the-top frilly and Frenchy. It's called La Cabinette.

So, where is this heading?

I often felt like I was abandoning my mother and my friends when we would go up there and stay for a week, even though it was only two hours away. I would call my mother every day, and I kept in constant contact with friends. If I didn't, I felt I had let them down. I can remember an instance when I called someone and they let me know they were too busy to talk! Obviously, I overrate my influence at times.

At the time though, I was hurt, until I realized, "Hey, they were just fine without me calling them every day." I had taken on far more responsibility for the relationship than was needed. It actually turned out to be very eye-opening for me. The relationship is even stronger now because I let go of my unrealistic expectations of myself as being the gatekeeper for any and all relationships in my life.

I've wasted a lot of days carrying burdens I didn't have to carry. I expect too much of myself. I always have. I doubt anyone has ever expected more of me than I have. Sound familiar?

It's a very common problem for those who are prone to depression. We generally place higher standards for ourselves than anyone else ever will. And it's wrong. When we do this, we are actually "thinking higher of ourselves than we should," as stated in Romans 12:3. We are not the world's gatekeepers.

So, it's a good idea to take a few minutes to put your self-expectations under a microscope and analyze them. Eventually, I realized that hanging on to such high self-standards served no useful purpose for my mother, my friends, or me. I learned to mentally prepare ahead of time by reminding myself it was only for a week, my brother lived with my mother, and I could get home in under two hours anyway.

I have always felt responsible for the happiness of those I love. It's truly unrealistic, and I know that, but I still fall back into those old patterns at times. I gave, and still give, myself far more power than any person has for the responsibility of another's happiness.

But then no one is responsible for mine either. That's a whole different lesson I had to learn.

The problem with ignoring our high self-expectation is that we can spiral into depression because we feel overburdened. I heard a saying a number of years ago, "There is a Savior, and you're not Him." Good to remember if you suffer from knight-on-a-white-horse syndrome.

We are also not our own Savior. As long as we expect that we have the power within us to make others happy, we will also believe that we can make ourselves happy. And while much of what I suggest in this book involves self-effort on our part, it also requires that we recognize that all healing ultimately comes from God.

It is not wrong to expect a great deal of ourselves. It's worse than not expecting enough. But when those self-expectations become too heavy and we absolve others from the responsibility for their lives, we take on more than we should. We are to bear one another's burdens, yes, but nowhere does scripture suggest we bear all of them ad infinitum.

We can learn to bring down our level of expectations, especially of ourselves. We can let others be human and make their mistakes. We can allow ourselves the same privilege.

Do you find yourself controlled by your self-expectations?

Is there a way you can bring down your level of self-expectations a little?

DAY 31
KNOW WHO AND WHOSE YOU ARE

> Will the clay say to the potter "What are you doing?"
> —Isaiah 45:9

It's surprising to me that people don't take the time to know themselves—who they are, what they like or don't like, talents and abilities, in other words, how the Potter designed their unique lump of clay.

Oh, wait. That was me at one time too. So, I guess it really isn't that surprising after all. While some people do have a degree of self-awareness, many don't.

I think it takes some self-reflection and some experimenting to find out who we are. When my mother was much older, she started to draw. She thought she was pretty bad, but I saw hidden talent and encouraged her. She never really got a chance to develop that gift though. I wonder what she could have done had someone encouraged her along the way or if she'd just thrown away her self-doubt long enough to try.

My mother came from an era when one never talked about self-reflection, and it might seem to be a little narcissistic to some people even now. But I don't think so. I think scripture supports this idea in Ephesians 3:20, that not only can we do more than we even imagine, we can also *be* more than we can imagine. The possibilities are endless. And it seems to me, the more we know ourselves, the more we can imagine and the more we can be.

We are at our best when we are living up to our greatest potential. But that means knowing who we are, our strengths and weaknesses, our talents and abilities, in other words, how the Potter shaped our clay.

There is a real danger if we don't pursue our gifts. I believe there are core talents and abilities in each of us that God has created, and they are meant to be developed. I believe we all have deep-seated interests and talents we need to unearth. Some of us know what those are, but because of our worry about how self-indulgent it sounds, we haven't pursued them. (My next book is all about this.) We need not ever apologize for pursing the dreams God has laid on our hearts. This is a time we singularly look to Jesus alone for approval. Should others come along, all the better. But if they don't, we have to remember who we are trying to honor.

It's also OK to be selfish about some things. I've purposefully/selfishly scheduled time to write and blog. I am purposefully/selfishly scheduling time for my art. And I purposefully/selfishly guard my quiet time with God. Let me share something about my own self-rediscovery during this pandemic.

I rediscovered my love of painting. I forgot how I can lose myself in the colors, the design, the creative process. I forgot how, when I'm truly absorbed in a creative project, my faith grows. It's like the creator in me has a symbiotic relationship with the Creator of all, and I experience God in a deeper way.

It could be any pursuit, because when we are genuinely in touch with ourselves, we just naturally feel closer to God. Think about that for a minute. *It's the clay feeling the hands of the Potter.*

Doesn't it make sense we would feel closer to God when we are living authentic lives? When we are being the person God created? When we are as close as possible to His design for us? When the clay accurately represents what the Potter fashioned?

In Jeremiah 18:6, God states, "Can I not, O house of Israel, deal with you as a potter does?" Although this verse is referring to God's sovereignty over nations, I think it also shows that we are wrong to fight against how the Potter has fashioned each of us. If He has given us talents and abilities, He intends for us to use them. There is nothing self-indulgent about knowing how we are molded by God.

We are much less apt to be depressed when we are engaged in those activities that bring us joy, when we are closer to representing that finished clay product that God fashioned at our inception.

What activity or hobby has sparked an interest in you? Will you take some time to research it?

DAY 32
ANXIETY AND DECISION-MAKING

> Do not be anxious about anything, but in every situation, by prayer and petition, with thanksgiving, present your requests to God. And the peace of God, which transcends all understanding, will guard your hearts and your minds in Christ Jesus.
> —Philippians 4:6–7

Everyone feels anxious now and then; that's normal. We feel anxious when we have a job interview, a public speaking engagement, before taking a test. Those are appropriate times to feel anxious, and the anxiety goes away once the stressful situation goes away.

Not so with anxiety disorders. This is a specific group of mental illnesses that keep you from living a normal life. Anxiety and depression often accompany each other; they can overlap and can even cause each other. Anxiety can also exist all on its own.

Anxiety is an awful feeling.

There are various versions and degrees of anxiety, but all can be disabling. The most common form is GAD, general anxiety disorder, and is characterized by a generalized fear and worry, meaning you can't name what you are anxious about; you are just anxious.

The common symptoms are panic, fear, disturbed sleep, heart

palpitations, muscle tension, shortness of breath, and heaviness in the chest, among others. If the heaviness in your chest is sudden, don't assume it is anxiety. See a doctor or visit an urgent care facility. Don't self-diagnose.

Antidepressants are often used to treat anxiety disorders as well as depression. Remember, symptoms of depression can mimic other health conditions. Again, don't self-diagnose.

We live in an anxious world. How could we not? Especially in the middle of a pandemic. We feel more fearful than ever because of all the uncertainty. Again, how could we not?

I love the fact that there is no guilt heaped on my head (yours either) in Philippians 4. There is also no limit to the number of times we can bring our anxiety to God. I would've already reached my max if there were!

But there is something we can do to limit the anxiety we feel, and it has to do with decision-making. We can try to eliminate unnecessary decision-making by putting some of our decisions on autopilot. There are so many decisions we make every day that we could streamline, thus reducing our anxiety levels.

We can plan menus and schedule household tasks so we don't get caught up in an endless loop of cleaning. We can organize better. We can build margin in our lives by allowing extra time to get from point A to point B. We only have so much emotional energy, and feeling overwhelmed because of too many decisions all the time uses up a lot of it. Fewer choices save some of it.

Decision-making is hard when we are anxious, and it uses a lot of energy, so why not try to make a lot of those decisions a habit so we don't even have to think about them?

When we're anxious, the fewer decisions we have to make the better. Simplifying and reducing the decisions we make can greatly help. We can make them habits instead of daily decisions.

Things like what time to go to bed and what time to get up. When to prepare meals, mow the lawn, and do household maintenance. Do your best not to vary from your schedule so that unfinished tasks don't pile up. Depression and anxiety respond extremely well to structure and routine.

If you want to make fewer decisions, make more decisions so automatic they become habitual.

Anxiety makes decision-making difficult. Sometimes it's not the act of making the decision as much as it is that anxiety produces such fear and dread we feel stuck and can't make a decision. We are afraid to move, much less decide something.

But remember, if you make a wrong decision, it can probably be corrected. Making no decision just keeps you in limbo. Besides, you can't learn from mistakes you don't make.

You need to reserve your emotional and mental energy for the decisions that really count. Save your brain power for the really important stuff.

Do you find yourself feeling anxious when having to make too many decisions?

Can you think of some you can put on autopilot?

DAY 33
WERE YOU BORN TOO OLD?

> Forget about what's happened. Don't keep going
> over old history ... I'm about to do something
> brand-new. It's bursting out! Don't you see it?
> —Isaiah 43:18–19 (MSG)

Some of us were just born old.

Asking us when we grew up is like asking us to solve a quantum physics equation in our head. We simply have no frame of reference. We've just always felt older than our years.

As children, we felt the weight of the world on our tiny shoulders, even though they weren't ready to carry such a load. Atlas may have shrugged it off, but we couldn't. Circumstances of our childhood conspired together in such a way to practically guarantee we would skip over some important stages. The sense of wonder, freedom, and innocence eluded us.

Fun became a four-letter word.

We see smiling pictures of ourselves in our parents' photo albums and don't recognize our own face because of those slapped-on-for-the-camera smiles. We do remember some good times, but we also remember fearing those moments would slip away too soon. And they usually did.

We knew those singular moments of happiness were like fireflies at night, hard to capture and even harder to keep alive.

If we could have put them in a jar to dip into in the future when needed, we would have. Those snippets of happiness weren't our real life; they were just cruel bits of what could be, what should be.

There is an old southern saying, "If you don't crawl before you walk, you will crawl before you die." I think it's supposed to mean that we are meant to experience certain phases in our lives at appropriate times, and if we don't, we will experience them inappropriately at other times in our lives.

Becoming an adult too soon is one of those "not crawling before we walk" kind of experiences. Doctors tell parents not to push their children to stand up too soon because their leg muscles haven't developed properly, and it could cause injury. The same is true for our emotions.

Some of us were forced to experience adulthood way ahead of schedule. Our underdeveloped emotional muscles were simply not ready to take on such mature themes. But we became very adept at carrying our burdens because we were survivors.

When life gets overwhelming now, we put on our big-girl or big-boy pants and tell ourselves, "Grow up, for crying out loud." The truth is we do a pretty good job; we have been trained well.

Depression can often be a result of growing up too fast. We skip all those normal, desirable, progressive stages crucial for good mental health. We are adults but with our child's needs unmet.

We can't recapture our childhoods, but we can certainly find our fun again. We can learn to play and laugh and just be silly for no reason. We can recapture that sense of childlike innocence every time we see a rainbow or the drops of water that form mirror-like drops on a Lady's Mantle plant. We can color in a coloring book or splash in a mud puddle.

I became a grown-up when I realized I could have fun, even pursue it intentionally. I now enjoy life without feeling guilty. I no longer feel I've ignored the suffering in the world just because I laugh.

If this sounds like your childhood, don't despair. It was mine too. But I've laughed a lot since then. I've had so much joy since then. I got a second chance at my childhood; it was just a little delayed.

Did you feel you grew up too soon?

Are you able to let the past go so you can find the joy that now awaits you?

DAY 34
IF WE WERE HAVING COFFEE

> There is no temptation (trial) that you are facing that has not been faced by others. But God is faithful and will not let you be tried or tested beyond what you are capable of handling with his help.
> —1 Corinthians 10:13 (my paraphrase)

I wish we could have coffee. I would love to have a conversation with each of you over a steaming latte.

I would truly get it if you told me you were suffering from depression. I would get it if you said you couldn't think of anything that caused it. I would get it if you told me all was right between you and God.

I would get it because as I write today, I find myself skirting the edge of the pit. But this is as close as I'm going to get.

I am putting into practice all the things that I know are right for me to do, like getting out of bed, making the bed, wearing nice clothes, doing my hair, having quiet time with God. I'm staying very busy. I'm writing. (And, of course, that could be a large part of it. You try writing about depression day in and day out.)

So, I get it, and I get it right now.

If you asked for my help today, here's what I would say to you (and it's exactly what I'm saying to myself):

1. Tell yourself you will get through this. I know, because I and millions of others have.
2. Remind yourself that you are stronger than you think you are. If you're feeling particularly weak right now, that doesn't mean you are. This is actually when you are the strongest. Why? Because God is showering extra grace on you.
"And he has said to me, My grace is sufficient for you, for power is perfected in weakness ... for when I am weak, then I am strong" (2 Corinthians 12:9–11).
3. Keep moving. Don't give in to lethargy. Trust me, I know how hard that is. Do something today you can feel good about tonight.
4. Talk to a trusted friend. It doesn't have to be in person, and if you don't want to talk about your depression, just tell someone you need prayers because you are struggling.
5. Stay in the spirit of prayer. Continuously focus on God. Give every negative thought to Him.
6. Rest. I know, right? I just got through telling you to stay busy, but there are times when you might need to stop and relax for an hour or so. Just make sure your thoughts rest as well.

If we were having coffee ...
I would tell you all the above.
I would pray with you.
I would let you know you are not less of a person because you are depressed.
I would let you know that God is with you in this battle.
I would probably cry as I heard your pain shouting through your words.
This is the same advice I give myself. I have written that there is *almost* always something that triggers our depression, and we

need to know what that is. But sometimes we search and search and simply can't figure it out.

Don't worry about it for now. You will eventually figure it out. Ask God to search your heart and your anxious thoughts. Remember, depression is often triggered by fear. Fear of losing someone you love. Fear of being alone. Fear of the unknown. Imagine Jesus confronting your fear and anxiety. What do you picture He would do with it?

Ask God to empower you to trust Him for the future.

"You are going to get better" is what I'd say if we we're having coffee.

What would you say to me if we were having coffee?
What would you say to someone else struggling with depression?

DAY 35

CHANGED RELATIONSHIPS

We improve the health of our relationships by improving our relationship with God first.

Sometimes when we start to get better, our relationships can suffer. You would think it would be just the opposite, wouldn't you?

If you've been depressed for long time, people are used to you as you once were. When you start to change, they might take some time adjusting to the new and improved you. You and the people around you have adopted certain roles during your depression, and those roles will most likely change.

Depression impacts our relationships, and getting better impacts our relationships as well, not always for the better. Some people may not understand the steps you need to take to improve your health.

Avoid any unnecessary drama at this point. If people say unkind things or discourage you when you try some new ways of thinking and acting, they probably just don't get the process. And if they don't, there is no way you will make them understand. Depression is very hard to understand if you've never been there yourself. Give them a break.

This is *your* journey to wholeness. Remind yourself that you are initiating changes because you are tired of feeling this way. You are not doing this to hurt anyone. For now, this is your journey, and you need to embrace this journey without apology.

Be patient with those people around you. And don't buy into

any drama for which you have no responsibility. Remember, if you have no responsibility in the conflict, "It's not your circus, and it's not your monkeys." Listen if appropriate, be kind, and pray, but let it remain with them.

Even though some of your relationships might change, that doesn't mean it's a bad change. Some of them might actually get better.

For example, if a spouse has been enabling and feeding their partner's depression, getting better will change that dynamic. They will no longer be the helper, the one to lean on. That might be difficult for them. The more independent you become, the more they might feel abandoned. Your relationships will find their own level of normal as you get better and those around you get used to the change.

Relationships are an important part of our recovery. More than likely, there were some unhealthy ones. But unhealthy relationships, just like healthy ones, are a part of all our lives. We can learn from both.

We can learn to make the good relationships better while backing away from the destructive ones that are not responding to our healthier selves. "If possible, so far as it depends on you live peaceably with all men" (Romans 12:18).

Some of your relationships might change. Your relationships will find their own level of normalcy as you get better and those around you get used to the change.

From my perspective, as I learned to manage and finally overcome my depression, I found I was allowing my family and friends the same freedom to be themselves that I now required. Even now, I work at allowing others to be who they are so I can be who I am.

Relationships are so much better that way.

What roles are your family and friends playing in your life? Can you see how some of these roles might need to change?

DAY 36

HEALTHY RELATIONSHIPS

> Put on a heart of compassion, kindness, humility, gentleness and patience, bearing with one another, and forgiving each other.
> —Colossians 3:12–13

Healthy relationships are important to our mental health. But remember, while we are created to be in relationship with others, no human relationship is meant to usurp our relationship with God.

There are some pretty unhealthy relationships throughout scripture. Sarah and Abraham had issues with fertility, and their solution—to use a concubine to have a child—certainly wasn't God's plan. David was not a good father to his daughter, Tamar, and had issues with his son Absalom. James was jealous of John. Peter thought he was the boss of everyone. Paul had issues with John Mark. They all had their unique relationship difficulties.

The truth is we are ignored and forgotten by our friends at times. Sometimes we are taken for granted. Sometimes we do the ignoring, the forgetting, and the taking for granted. We are not the perfect spouse, parent, and friend. Thank goodness we don't have to be, because perfection is hard to maintain.

At the same time, relationships always involve at least two people, so we don't have to take all the responsibility or all the blame if it goes south. The success or failure of a relationship doesn't always depend on us, but some of us who are the overly responsible type think it does.

We need relationships that nurture us when we need nurturing, that challenge us when we need challenging, and most certainly that inspire us to develop a closer relationship with God. So maybe we need a yardstick to measure what that looks like for us. Maybe we even need to write down what we consider are the parameters of healthy relationships, especially for future ones.

For me, it's authenticity, reciprocity, and lack of jealousy. Make up your own list; it helps keep your focus when making new friendships. You notice I didn't mention faith. While my deepest relationships are with those who do share my faith, I wouldn't want to exclude someone because of that.

Relationships take a lot of emotional and physical energy.

Even with those parameters, however, we have to remember that not everyone is going to display every one of those qualities all the time. And neither are we. We are one half of every relationship we have. While we can't meet all of our family's and friends' needs, we have to remember that they can't meet all ours either.

We have all probably let down the people we love. We have also been let down by those who love us. That's life. It's when we expect more of others than they are willing or capable of giving that causes issues.

When we expect others to make us happy, we run into trouble. When others expect us to make them happy, we run into trouble as well.

Only God is able to meet all our needs, and He may even require we meet a few of our own.

Relationship difficulties are often a precursor to depression, so it only makes sense to have the healthiest ones we can.

Are you looking for people to meet all your needs?
Are you looking for people to make you happy?

DAY 37
WHAT IS A GOOD FRIENDSHIP?

> When we spend too much time wanting who we
> want, the who one wants us gets ignored.

Sometimes we delegate friendships to the back burner because there is no family blood coursing through their veins.

That is a huge mistake.

Good friends can often understand our depression in ways that family members can't. They can be a shoulder to cry on when we need it and a poke in our ribs to get us moving as well. Our histories with our friends are not as tangled as our family histories. There is usually some distance.

But at times, we try to hang onto a friendship that was never what we thought it was in the first place. We just wanted it so much we overlooked a lot. We never questioned whether it was a friendship God sanctioned. I believe God wants us to have friendships that are meaningful and reciprocal. We can certainly have relationships that are not reciprocal, but a friendship should always be that way.

I hit it off with someone at our first encounter and pursued the relationship. I invited her to coffee. I stopped by her house a number of times. She really seemed to enjoy our time together. After a few months, I thought, *Wait, a minute. She has never reciprocated, not even once. Hmm, think I'll see what happens if I just stop for a while.* (I am not a high-maintenance friend. I don't expect if I make a phone call, a phone call has to returned before I call again. But I do expect general reciprocity.)

I had no doubt she liked me and enjoyed our friendship but not to the point she was willing to work at it. I backed off to see if she would lean forward. She didn't. So I simply let the friendship die its natural death. The funeral was short and the grieving even shorter, especially for her. Although I didn't regret the friendship we enjoyed, I was just not willing to carry the responsibility for all of it anymore.

When she finally caught on that I wasn't calling anymore, we had a conversation about the demise. She admitted she was bad at keeping in touch and expressed sadness over the end of our friendship but gave no indication anything would change. I accepted her apology. We are still friendly when we see each other, and I check in on her once in a while. But I no longer pursue a deep relationship with her.

Jesus had three really close friends. *Only three.* Not everyone has to be our bestie. This is not to suggest that we casually walk away from a friendship, especially a long-term one, just because we run into a rough patch. Applying a measuring stick occasionally to gauge where we are and where we seem to be going keeps us on track and keeps the relationship healthy.

God has all kinds of reasons for putting people in our paths, and even when a relationship goes south, God is teaching us something. One of those things might be this: never make someone a priority in your life when they only make you an option in theirs. Or, as I like to say, don't make someone an exclamation point in your life when you are only a comma in theirs.

However, when we are seriously depressed is not the time to apply that yardstick. Make no decisions about friendships when you are feeling really low. In fact, during a depressive episode is no time to make any life-altering decisions about any relationship—or anything else for that matter. Depression has an uncanny way of making us doubt every relationship we have anyway. That's the enemy's plan.

And remember, we don't need—nor should we have—intimate friendships with everyone we meet. Relationships fit different aspects of who we are and what our interests are, and the deepest friendships have a shared faith.

There is only one who can serve that perfect-relationship need, and He never disappoints or fails to return our call.

Do you have a friendship that needs some readjusting?

Can you try talking to God as if He was your best friend? Because guess what? He is.

DAY 38

RELATIONSHIPS: THE SEQUEL

> Wounds from a friend can be trusted,
> but an enemy multiplies kisses.
> —Proverbs 27:5–6

(Because relationships are so important, whether depressed or not, but especially when depressed, I am giving this subject more time.)

Who are the people you are most comfortable with? They should be your closest connections during your healing process. If you're not comfortable sharing your struggles with long-term friends, you need to ask why.

Take time every so often to think about your relationships with the people in your life. If some seem to be waning, is it them or could it be you? Ask yourself if there are some things you can do to make those relationships better, realizing of course that you can only do so much.

Be willing to let some relationships, like water, find their own level. I'm one of those people with an overly developed conscience. I take way too much responsibility for others' happiness. Are you like that?

Quit being the first one to initiate that phone call or that cup of coffee. See what happens when you step back. Sometimes we rob our friends of an opportunity to take some responsibility for the relationship because we keep doing it for them. When we allow them some time to come forward, they either will or they won't. For the ones who won't, there's your sign. If they choose to let the relationship slide, there is nothing you can do about it.

If your current relationships aren't working out, seek new ones. Join a book club or a Bible study. Initiate coffee with a coworker. Join an advocacy group about something you are passionate about. There are all kinds of ways to meet people. Everyone needs a friend. It's a happy occurrence when your needs and their needs form a mutual pairing of strengths and weaknesses.

Be willing to forgive. While there are some relationships that need to settle, there are others we need to nurture due to the length of the relationship. We love them, and they love us, but something has gotten in the way. Have an honest and loving conversation. Be willing to forgive and be willing to ask for forgiveness. A long-term friend is a friend to treasure. They are few and far between.

Give the friends in your life some space. You might not always get what they're going through, but love them anyway. None of us gets it right all the time.

At the same time, be an authentic person. Don't be afraid to be who you are. Don't pretend all is well if it isn't. There should be a wide place for you both to walk. Give them grace and give yourself some grace as well.

Avoid bitter, negative, toxic people as much as you can. If you live with one, close your ears and walk away if you can. If that isn't possible, make sure you have a trusted person you can talk to when it gets overwhelming. Follow an inspirational blog that lifts your spirits.

A word of caution about blogs. Some of them are nothing more than a dumping ground, with everyone sharing their story but no one making any strides to get better. Follow blogs where people are willing to share their struggles but are doing their part to get healthy.

Pray about every important relationship in your life. Ask God for insight. Healthy relationships are so important to our overall well-being. Keep yours healthy "as much as it depends on you" (Romans 12:18).

Can you think of a relationship for which you take too much responsibility?

Is there a relationship where you are the one not doing enough?

DAY 39

WHO IS WRITING YOUR STORY?

> But Daniel made up his mind.
> —Daniel 1:8

Who is writing your story?

I think of so many stories in scripture about people whose story was written *for* them and those who wrote their *own* story. It's not that the former had no choice but to let the story be written for them; it's that they abdicated being their own author.

I think of Daniel especially as someone who wrote his own story from the very beginning. He is one of my superheroes. From the beginning of his captivity, he was the one doing the writing. His determination and resolve always inspire me. He didn't write just the beginning of his story; he wrote the whole thing, right to the end.

From the very first chapter of Daniel, we see his determination to remain true to God. No one else was going to tell him what to eat or drink. And he was smart about it. He was even a little political. He had gained the favor of one of the chief officials, but that official was afraid to go along with Daniel's idea. So, Daniel talked to the next person down the hierarchy, the guard.

When you're writing your own story, you have to make good decisions all along the way, and Daniel did just that.

He convinced the guard to let him and his friends eat only

fruits and vegetables for ten days and then asked to be compared to the other young men brought from Babylon who were eating the royal food. As it turned out, Daniel and his friends were far healthier after those ten days and as a result gained favor with Nebuchadnezzar.

Daniel and his friends were the heroes of their own story.

Jonah, on the other hand, was someone who never wrote his own story and instead let his jealousy and anger so consume him that when we read his story, we certainly don't see a hero. In fact, his last recorded words, when asked by God whether he had a right to be angry, were "I do. I am angry enough to die." What a way to be remembered, huh?

Up to a certain point in our lives, our stories were written for us by our parents. But each of us comes to a place in our lives where we become the authors of our story (with God's direction, of course). We write the plot. No one else does.

How do we want our story to read? If your life was currently being written by someone monitoring your movements, thoughts, and words, how would your story look? Will someone read your story and be encouraged and inspired, or will they say, "That's such a sad story."

What is your plot? Do you have one? Meaning, do you know your purpose in life? You have one, you know. We all do. As we find that purpose and start fulfilling it, we begin to be our own author.

Our purpose doesn't have to be spectacular or out of the ordinary. I would suggest that for most people, it has more to do with the caring and nurturing of the people in their lives rather than accomplishing some great feat. It doesn't matter how exciting your story is, only that you are the one writing it.

For me, I came to a place where I simply had to determine the theme of the story in which I was the main character. The way it was heading, it could have been one of those melodramas full of tears, where we leave the theater feeling worse than when we entered. We feel sorry for the heroine because we saw the sad ending coming from the very beginning.

I decided early on that I preferred to be the heroine in an inspirational story rather than the villain in a dark drama. Besides, heroines are always pretty, and wicked witches have warts on their noses.

Who is writing your story?
When will you start writing it yourself?

DAY 40
WHY BOUNDARIES ARE GOOD

> Set up for yourself roadblocks. Place for yourself guidepost; direct your mind to the highway.
> —Jeremiah 31:21

I love this verse. I find it so freeing. I like the feeling it conveys, that my road is protected by these guideposts like the railings on curvy roads high in the mountains. I like the image of directing my mind to the highway. It keeps me focused.

Sometimes we think of boundaries as something we do to keep others away. But boundaries are meant for more than just that. They are also meant for self-preservation.

That's what Jeremiah is saying. This is one of my favorite verses. It is the one I always refer to when I need to really focus on something. I find it very encouraging.

We set boundaries so we feel freer to pursue God's call in our lives. We establish boundaries so we can protect our time and our emotional energy.

When we let others constantly bombard us with their issues, and we never see them doing anything constructive, they drain our emotional energy. We don't have an unlimited supply. We need to conserve it.

We need to set up boundaries for what we will allow to come into our lives and what we won't. We especially need to set up boundaries for negative and destructive people. We need to have parameters in place for those people and know when to walk away. I wasn't very good at it, and that could have contributed to my depression.

There's only so much negativity you should allow into your life as you heal from depression. This doesn't mean you cut people out of your life; it just means you monitor their effect on you.

There was a woman like that in my life. I knew to never talk to her in the morning because she was so disagreeable. I never initiated a morning conversation with her, and if she called me, I always found a reason to get off the phone as soon as possible. It greatly helped our relationship.

When I began finally finishing this book, I set up some soft boundaries as well. I did that by intentionally scheduling time for the people in my life during times I wasn't writing. I didn't want to damage any relationships by ignoring them. If things didn't work out for us to get together, I let it go and no longer felt a sense of guilt because I knew I had tried.

But let me be clear. I would quickly tear down any boundary for a person in real need, and certainly for friends and family. As Christians, we are called to do that. A person in real crisis is a person for whom boundaries don't apply.

By the way, Jesus often set up boundaries. He left his disciples to go pray. They weren't invited. He didn't attend a festival when the disciples wanted him to. He didn't immediately respond to Mary and Martha when they sent a message saying their brother was deathly ill. He didn't put himself in harm's way until He was ready.

These boundaries weren't because Jesus didn't want to be around people. Hardly. Jesus set them up because He had to be about His Father's business at the Father's right time.

We need some boundaries in our faith walk as well. Are we sabotaging our time with God by not setting up personal boundaries to prevent infringement on that time? I could be doing any number of other things today, but I have purposely established some boundaries in my life this week so I will finish this book. Everything else is on the back burner. A back burner is a good boundary because it can be turned on and off easily.

But boundaries are not set in stone. They're *our* boundaries, and they change as our lives change. A necessary boundary today may not be needed tomorrow. And where we don't have one now, we may need one in the future.

Remember, boundaries are a positive, not a negative, and are intended to help, not hurt.

Do you need to establish some boundaries?
What are they?

DAY 41
STATISTICS ARE NOT YOUR DESTINY

> In Christ, he is a new creature (person); the old has passed away.
> —2 Corinthians 5:17

Maybe this is your second, third, or even fourth go-around with depression.

I bet you've been told that you'll probably always have depressive episodes because of certain statistics. And while some statistics do suggest that once you experience depression, you are twice as likely to experience a second episode, it's not carved in stone. Many mental health professionals say that with each successive episode, the percentage gets higher, and pretty soon, you can look forward to always being depressed.

Nice, huh? Nothing like setting someone up for failure.

You have probably also heard that the tendency toward experiencing depression is much higher if you have a family history of it. OK, let's look at this.

Just because family members struggle with weight issues, for example, does that guarantee you will? You can make better food and beverage choices. You can exercise daily. You can live an all-around healthier lifestyle.

My mother experienced life-depleting depression her entire life. I don't. Why? Different lifestyles, different choices. Plus, I was willing to work hard.

If your coping mechanisms, your worldview, your thought processes, and your habits all contributed or even caused your depression, and you have made significant positive changes in those areas, why would you have another episode?

If medication caused it and you no longer take that medication, why would you have another episode? Or if you had a medical illness that caused it, and that illness is no longer there, why would you still be depressed?

If everyone in this world lived their life based on statistics regarding their age, gender, education, and all the other limiting numbers out there, this would be a sad world because only those who the statistics favored would accomplish any great feats. And yet there are a lot of people who, sadly, never rise to accomplish the greatness they were designed for because they believe the numbers.

Statistics are not destiny. Statistics are not your destiny.

Statistics are just numbers. Numbers don't make choices. Numbers don't mature or change. Numbers don't have a God. Numbers are just numbers.

And remember, God can work miracles. He can deliver anyone from anything. What were the odds, the numbers, that a man from an ill-thought-of town could change the world? Not just change the world but become the Savior of the world? Jesus certainly beat all the odds, even death.

Should you at least pay attention to the numbers? Sure. Forewarned is forearmed. But don't assume that you will always be the victim of such predictions. If members of your family experience depression, by all means take that into account—and then beat the odds.

God is able to beat every statistic, every time. (Trust me on this one.)

When my husband and I married, because of our families' dysfunctions, the stats were all against us having a successful marriage. Our friends made good-hearted bets we wouldn't make it. Seriously, they did. The very day of our wedding, they did. Some friends, huh? Frankly, we had given them lots of ammunition to think that way, so we weren't offended.

But we vowed to make our marriage work *despite those statistics*. And we did. With God's help, we did.

You do not have to fall victim to some statistic telling you that you are doomed to always struggle with depression. You are more than a number. You are a new creature in Christ with a whole new future other than one some statistician laid out for you.

Have you been told you will never get better?
Will you try to beat the odds?

DAY 42

DON'T IGNORE YOUR FEELINGS

> The heart is more deceitful than all else. And is desperately sick—who can understand it?
> —Jeremiah 17:9

Depressed or not, most of us would do well to understand the mental and emotional connection between what we think and say and how that affects our overall mental health.

Many people put on a good front. To listen to them, you would think everything is wonderful, even though you know it isn't. They believe their own lies. Most of us know people like that. If you were to peek inside their heart, when there isn't a wall of words protecting it, you would find a person in need. I know that to be true because God said it in Jeremiah.

That verse in Jeremiah is not meant to condemn us. Nothing in God's Word is meant to condemn us, but it is to remind us that we all have those secret, destructive places in our heart that even we don't know exist. It's those places where depression and anxiety lurk, waiting to pounce.

When we are confronted with certain people and certain circumstances, thoughts come into our head, and words spew out of our mouth that surprise even us. That's the parts of our heart where our prejudices, our judgmental and sanctimonious attitudes, and our innate selfishness dwell. We should never say, "Whoa, that wasn't like me!"

Yes, it was. It's just like all of us. Given the right circumstances, we can all succumb to the worst in us. To suggest otherwise denies reality and says Jeremiah was wrong.

Most of the time, we have no idea what are the origins of our feelings; we just know they are there. Other times, we know exactly where they come from. Overwhelming research agrees that feelings always start from a specific source, and that's our thoughts.

But we shouldn't ignore our feelings; they tell us a great deal about ourselves. We need to admit to them and correctly identify them so we don't fall victim to them.

No matter how much we think we are in touch with our feelings, we still experience great difficulty controlling them. Depression-prone people, because of the very nature of the illness, have a greater tendency to harbor unhealthy feelings toward themselves, than other people. However, our emotions don't have to rule over us. We don't have to be at their mercy.

As with many facets of depression, feelings can be a symptom and/or a cause. Let resentful, angry feelings build up (cause), and we are often dragged down to depression (symptom). It works the other way around as well. Let depression build up (cause), and we can often become angry (symptom). Were we to deal with either cause early on, we could stop the cycle.

Our feelings originate from within us, not from outside sources. There is no outside force making us feel a particular way. No one person has the power to make us feel anything. We always have a choice about our feelings.

Certainly, there may be precipitating factors. Some situations we find ourselves in are very hurtful. It certainly does no good to deny them, but not every hurt feeling needs to be addressed. Acknowledged to ourselves, yes; addressed, no. Sometimes we simply have to overlook them and get on with our lives.

Besides, how does it benefit you to hang on to those feelings? Does it change the situation?

Hurt feelings, like a festering sore, will just keep oozing into all parts of our life unless they are cauterized.

We've often heard that we shouldn't trust our feelings. That's true. Feelings, like thoughts, are not always based on facts. Sometimes they are. But we absolutely must pay attention to them. They are bullhorns that are shouting to us about the condition of our heart and mind.

Our feelings tell us a lot about us.

Do you often find yourself out of touch with your feelings? What does this tell you?

DAY 43

ARE YOU TAKING VITAMIN G?

> Giving thanks always and for everything to God the
> Father in the name of our Lord Jesus Christ.
> —Ephesians 5:20

Have you heard of vitamin G? Vitamin G is gratitude.

I think this is probably the hardest concept for a depressed person to wrap their heads around. When we're depressed, we feel anything but grateful. That thing we should be grateful for could be sitting right in front of us (it usually is), and we wouldn't see it. That's how depression messes with our mind. Our blessings are hidden under the shroud of darkness.

I remember those days well. I knew I should be grateful for all God had done, so I would utter the words but feel like a fraud. I knew my words were a little insincere. But I finally came to realize that whether or not I felt like it, I needed to speak them anyway. Nothing changes the truth that there is always something to be thankful for. Whether it feels fraudulent or not, we need to use our words and speak gratitude into the world.

The truth is we all have some thing or someone to be grateful for. If not today, then in the past. Good has come our way, in some way, at some time. Someone, somewhere has been kind to us. It's the rare individual for whom this would not be true. And if that is true, I hope our collective hearts break and prompt us to extend kindness to everyone.

One of the subtle triggers for depression is not regularly maintaining a grateful heart, and we can easily fall out of the habit of doing it if we're not being vigilant.

An acquaintance of mine from our church posted something on her Facebook page as I was writing this book that is really appropriate here. She agreed to let me tell her story.

Jan is truly a spirit-led Christian. She has a wonderful servant's heart. She had a jail ministry for many years. Jan had struggled often with depression and wrote that it seemed to be returning. As she was questioning why, she realized that she had inadvertently quit doing the one thing that she felt had helped her greatly in the past.

And that was expressing gratitude.

She said she started thanking God again every day for something or someone, and eventually her depression started to lift. She went on to state that she found it interesting that she *knew* this was an important part of keeping her depression at bay, but she had just quit doing it. It wasn't that she had decided not to; but like so many things, it had just slipped away due to negligence.

There are some things we just have to express no matter how we feel. Gratitude is one of them.

I used to have a small red bowl I kept in our bathroom. It was full of stones, and on the stones were written just one word, "Remember." On the back was the reference to Joshua 4. Joshua commanded the twelve men who represented the twelve tribes of Israel to gather up a stone for each tribe as a remembrance of God's faithfulness to them.

Remembering is a good prompt for us as well. Remember all God has done in the past for you and express thanks.

Gratitude has to be expressed, or it's not really gratitude anyway, is it?

In Philippians 4:6, the apostle Paul tells us to bring our

anxiety, and I would add *depression*, to God, and God will provide the peace we so desperately seek. And here's how we bring it: *with thanksgiving*. Thanksgiving (gratitude) is the prerequisite for peace and thus deliverance from depression and anxiety.

So, if you are struggling with this, take your vitamin G. I take one every day.

Thank God that you can bring your anxiety to Him. There's your vitamin G. If you can find nothing else to be grateful for today, be grateful for that, that the God of the universe invites you to bring your anxiety/depression to Him.

How much vitamin G are you taking?

Can you begin to thank God every day for something or someone?

DAY 44

LONELINESS

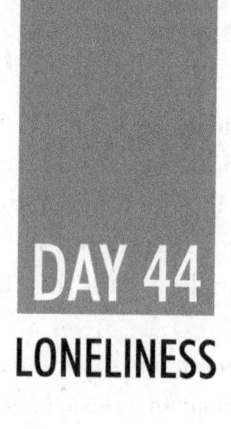

Turn to me and be gracious to me, for I am lonely and afflicted.
—Psalm 25:16

I can vividly remember the sense of loneliness I experienced in my depression. It was a terrible feeling. I felt isolated and distant from everyone. I felt like no one saw me, even when I was right in front of them. I would go grocery shopping and feel invisible (not so bad if I looked terrible).

Feeling lonely is a feeling of being totally alone in this world, even when there are people all around. It's a frightening and overwhelming feeling. Loneliness takes our mind to the ultimate conclusion: "We are alone in this world. No one cares about us."

We like to think our suffering is unique, that our loneliness is unique. But no matter how lonely you are, there is someone else feeling just as lonely. It's a false assumption to think only we suffer loneliness. Loneliness is universal. The more we connect via social media rather than in person, the more loneliness we experience. And with this pandemic, all the more so.

But you are not the only lonely person. It just feels that way. You'd be surprised how, when you reach out to someone, you learn they have periods of loneliness as well. We all do.

Sometimes we are lonely because we have pushed people

away. We've placed such high expectations in a relationship that people have walked away from us.

Expect the best in people, and you will attract people to you. When you meet someone, show a sincere interest in them by asking them about themselves. Most people love to have someone show an interest in them. Personally, I like getting to know people and their stories.

Facebook can really trigger a feeling of loneliness. Seriously. We go to our home page, and there are all those pictures of people with family and friends, and everyone is smiling and laughing. Ouch! But think about it for a minute. Why would they post anything else? Most of us don't post about the bad stuff. Do you?

None of us want to experience FOBLO, fear of being left out. But social media triggers that response in us. We want to be part of the fun crowd.

Social media is not real life. Down deep, we all know that, but we still get sucked in. There are many who are trying to make their life more exciting than it is. What you are seeing is only a quick snapshot of their day. You have no idea what the rest of their life looks like. Maybe it is as wonderful as it appears, and frankly, let's hope it is. We should want that for everyone. But maybe it's not, and this is how they deal with it.

But then there is *aloneness*. Jesus was alone the moment He started his ministry. There wasn't one human being that *got* Him. How could they? And yet there is no indication Jesus was sad about His aloneness. In fact, He often made sure He was alone. He knew joy in His aloneness. He embraced His aloneness.

There is a difference between aloneness and loneliness. We need to embrace aloneness. Aloneness can bring a wonderfully contented sense of peace. It is often in aloneness we find ourselves.

Perhaps we've made loneliness a bigger problem than it needs to be because we haven't learned how to handle our aloneness. If we're uncomfortable being alone, that's an indication we are not friends with ourselves. And it's perfectly OK to like our own company. Me and myself are quite good friends for the most part.

Aloneness can be rather calming and insightful. Loneliness, on the other hand, can be a catalyst to seek out God's presence. In our loneliest, we learn firsthand what it means to have a friend closer than a brother.

How do you handle being by yourself?
Do you automatically call it loneliness?

DAY 45
THE CETH PROGRAM

> Happiness is probably the easiest emotion to feel, the most elusive to create deliberately, and the most difficult to define.
> —Norman Cousins

In case you're wondering, CETH (my own creation) stands for the Christian's Entitlement to Happiness Program, meaning that Christians often feel entitled to happiness.

Most researchers now agree there are four basic emotions: happiness, sadness, fear, and anger. Some include others. When I looked at those others, I felt they all fit under one of the four main types. We will look at happiness first. (Note, happiness is not a separate section in the toolbox because happiness doesn't need a tool, does it? Managing your destructive and negative thoughts, words, and actions will result in a happier state of mind anyway.)

We feel like failures as Christians if we dare admit our lives aren't wonderful. I mean, haven't you met some Christians who are so bubbly and sweet and full of Jesus talk that they almost make you cringe a little? Just being honest here.

I've known a few myself. Their lives are as much a mess as anyone else's, yet they act as though they don't have a care in the world. And you know that's not true. They simply refuse to admit they have struggles like the rest of us. For them to admit to it might cause us to think they're not super Christians.

Frankly, I'm always drawn to real Christians, not the syrupy sweet ones. As my proper British friend says, "It's like having too much sugar in your tea." I don't mean to be snarky about this, but I do think many people who struggle with depression feel condemned when they encounter these attitudes. It's that whole comparison thing, which should never exist among believers, anyway.

Seeing as Jesus certainly faced His own struggles and never pretended He didn't, I wonder why some of us do. Besides, where do we find that Jesus promised us a life free of problems? In fact, didn't He say just the opposite? And yet we feel entitled to happiness.

It is often said that there is this vacuum in each of us that only God can fill. I agree, but what should be added is that that vacuum might not be *completely* filled this side of heaven. The visions of heaven recorded in Revelation paint such a beautiful and blissful picture. It's truly the carrot at the end of the stick.

At times, it seems cruel to read there will be no more tears in heaven when we're crying buckets down here. When we read there will be no more pain when we walk through those gates, that promise seems the greatest pain of all when our pain on earth is so severe.

And the pain of depression certainly qualifies for severe.

Haven't you ever, like the apostle Paul, felt a desire to be in heaven? Sometimes we just want to experience everything Revelation describes, even the downright scary-looking creatures. I know they are described as beautiful, but frankly, I don't see it.

I've experienced many wonderfully happy days, far more than I probably deserve. However, I don't assume for one minute that I am guaranteed these days. I wish I were. I wish we all were. If I could give happiness away to everyone, I would.

There are days I feel really burdened for the people I love and the struggles they face. It's at those times though that I remind myself I'm on this earth so I can intercede for them.

Yes, it would be great if every day was a happy day. But every day can be a joy-filled day when we rely on God and remember that we are promised peace but not necessarily happiness.

I've often said happiness is overrated. Happiness is often fleeting and depends on our circumstances. But real joy and contentment are not subject to the winds of change, because God is ever persistent and ever consistent. He is the one who "rides on the wings of the wind" (Psalm 104:3).

Do you try to pretend that things are always good in your life? Why do you think that is?

DAY 46
GETTING A GRIP ON ANGER

> When Haman saw that Mordecai would not bow down
> or show him respect, he was filled with rage.
> —Esther 3:5

Anger, demonstrated wrongly, is the most destructive emotion of all. However, it is appropriate when it prompts justice. It is often the catalyst for the development of organizations that bring relief and assistance to those in need. Mothers Against Drunk Driving (MADD) certainly began because of righteous anger.

And there are times anger can be a motivator. I can remember in my own struggle with depression that I eventually got just plain mad about it. I told myself, "I'm done with this! I am not letting depression take even one more day of my life!"

But let's be honest. Our anger is usually the garden variety type.

Many mental health professionals say depression is anger turned inward. Very often, anger starts in childhood because a child does not have the emotional maturity to handle their anger or the anger of the adults in the home. Sometimes they've not been allowed to express it, so they stuff it deep inside, where it festers and eats at their very soul. As adults, they are not aware that anger is behind a lot of behavior. They appear very docile and accommodating, while all the time the cauldron is boiling.

Anger is generally only the tip of the iceberg. A person who is always angry is often using their anger to hide their hurt. Anger is often a subterfuge for other emotions, such as disappointment, frustration, and hurt.

When we are angry about something, that feeling of anger is telling us something about ourselves. We need to examine its causes.

Are we angry about what we say we are angry about? Or have our frustrated feelings over the past few days escalated and we've exploded about some irrelevant event?

When the Bible states, "Don't let the sun go down on your anger" (Ephesians 4:26), it means far more than just not going to bed angry. It implies that if you go to bed angry, you will wake up angry, and the whole cycle starts all over again. It means, "Stop it!" for your own well-being and your own mental health.

While righteous anger against racism, intolerance, and injustice is a motivator for change, some people don't express even this type of anger as they should. They end up doing more harm than good. We can all learn to express our righteous anger with well-chosen, noninflammatory words.

When we are angry, who are we angry with anyway? In the final analysis, it's God, isn't it?

Count to ten before you express your anger. That old advice is still some of the best there is. If that doesn't work, find something that does. Walk away. Take a deep breath. Pinch yourself. You get the idea. Develop a personal strategy.

Remember how you felt when someone blurted out angry words at you? How did it make you feel? You immediately recoiled, didn't you? We get scared, befuddled. "Where did that come from?" you said in bewilderment.

It takes a very long time to get past hurtful words. I'm not talking about those arguments when we disagree vehemently about the issues of the day. Those are important conversations to have. I'm also not referring to the arguments when, once the air is cleared, a mutual understanding is reached. That is how all arguments should end.

I am referencing those angry words that bring up the past, that label people, that are purposefully meant to hurt. Fractions caused by this kind of anger can destroy a relationship, even causing generational splits among families than can last a lifetime.

If you are an angry person, get some help. Don't destroy your life or anyone else's.

You own your anger, not anyone else.

Do you think you are an angry person?
What are you angry about?

DAY 47
SADNESS

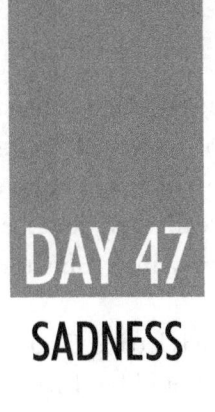

> You cannot protect yourself from sadness without protecting yourself from happiness.
> —Johnathon Foer

In order to feel sadness, we have to feel happiness, and to feel happiness, we have to feel sadness. It's a mixed bag, and to experience one means we need to experience the other.

Sadness is a perplexing emotion because we don't always know what we are sad about. We are just sad. Conversely, it's our capacity to feel sad that makes us empathetic. But when everything makes us sad and we are sad much of the time, that's a good indicator we are depressed.

Continual sadness is a common symptom of depression.

Sadness is also often accompanied or caused by loneliness. Loneliness is on the increase especially because of the pandemic which I referred to earlier. Yet we are "connecting" frequently with others via social media. It's no newsflash that social media can isolate us and that nothing takes the place of face-to-face interaction. Certainly, social distancing isn't helping.

Reach out to friends when you have these feelings. Even a phone call makes a difference. But what else can you do about your sadness?

It's easy to say, "Think about good things." My husband just told me he reminds himself when he is sad that he has no reason to be sad and moves on. At first, I thought that sounded a little too cut and dried, like when someone says, "Just get over it." But that approach can really help for fleeting feelings of sadness. Distraction also effectively interrupts those feelings as does any type of exercise.

And, of course, there is letting God in on our sadness. I'm not as good about that as I should be. I let my sadness grow before I lay it at His feet. What a waste of time.

One day last summer, I found myself feeling sad because a friend had not followed through on our plans to get together, although they were nebulous plans at best. I was overwhelmed from writing this book, and I was looking forward to stepping away from it and having iced tea with her on my deck.

Instead of giving her the benefit of a doubt, I took that sadness and transformed it from a hill to a mountain. I set myself up for a fall. I realized it almost immediately and quickly turned around my thinking. My big thing became a much smaller thing, and I started to feel better.

Today, I feel a little sad. We are just coming out of a pandemic, there is civil and international unrest But that sadness doesn't derail me because I can identify the source of my sadness.

And that brings me to this:

Get to the source of your sadness. If you are struggling with depression, feelings of sadness are very common. Don't be afraid to call it what it is. When we identify our emotions correctly, we take the first step to getting better.

Sometimes we feel ashamed of our sadness. We think it makes us look too needy. But you know what? Everybody is needy at various times, and the smart person, the one who wants to eliminate unnecessary sadness, will do things to bring joy into their lives.

Remember that friend I mentioned earlier? She could tell by my voice I was upset. She immediately called back and said she

DEPRESSION HAS A BIG VOICE

was hopping in the shower and would be over shortly. Here's my confession.

I wish I would have come right out and said, "I'm feeling kind of sad and overwhelmed and just wanted to talk to you." After she came over, I did. She said she knew, and that's why she came.

Don't be afraid to express your sadness and your needs to the important people in your life.

Do you find yourself feeling sad more than you want?
Do you think you could tell someone?

DAY 48

UNRELENTING FEAR

> When I am afraid, I will trust in you.
> —Psalm 56:3

Another basic emotion is fear.

I've thought hard about this. While I offer tools for dealing with fear in the toolbox, and while most of the time they work, I can remember times when nothing seemed to help. My fear and anxiety are rooted in my childhood. I went to bed anxious and afraid and woke up in the same state.

There are times when the fear and anxiety just refuse to go away. They grab our heart and squeeze it so hard we can't breathe. We feel like we are suffocating. So, what can we do?

Do whatever works. Sometimes it's prayer. Sometimes it's distraction. Sometimes it's movement. And sometimes it's just giving in to it and admitting it's going to be a tough day, and you just have to deliberately place one heavy foot in front of the other.

Let's face it. Sometimes you just have to learn to live with some fear. There are more than two hundred verses of scripture about fear. But you know the best part? Those verses never suggest the fear goes away for good. I find that comforting in a strange way. I guess that's why there *are* two hundred plus verses. We just have to keep on addressing it.

Fear is often rooted in childhood, especially trauma. We

become hardwired to feel fear as our first response to any threatening situation, no matter how much that situation is based on false premises. Fear and anxiety are kissing cousins. Our anxiety is closely tied to fear.

And fear of a returning depression is one of the worst. If you've ever been clinically depressed, you don't ever want to go there again. It's your worst nightmare.

In the course of writing this devotional, I had a couple of periods where I was sure my depression, after twenty years of recovery, was nipping at my heels again. I went back on some medication for a short period but then decided to fend off the impending depression using the tools I had developed. I took myself in hand and read everything I'd written over the years for this book.

Even though I know it's true, it still bewilders me that an illness as crippling as depression can be eased and managed in such simple ways. But it can. Something as simple as quick prayer of gratitude can help. Or setting out a pretty placemat and sitting down and eating a real breakfast.

Maybe it's precisely because we've quit doing the simple things. Maybe it's because we haven't been treating ourselves like real human beings who deserve to have a pretty placemat or a specialty coffee from our favorite barista. Maybe it's because we've forgotten what makes us feel good.

I don't know why the simple things work, only that they do, especially if you fear an impending episode.

If you're reading this book and are worried that you are headed down that road, try not to panic. Think back to how you managed to come out of the last episode. If you don't know how you recovered then, now is the time to develop some strategies, which is what my toolbox is all about.

Fear of a returning depression is very real. It makes you catch your breath as though someone has startled you. It's virtually impossible to explain to anyone who hasn't been there.

Don't let the fear of depression bring on a real episode.

Stay away from that pit by reminding yourself that God knows, understands, and accepts your fear. God knows that fear is a big problem for us. Remember, there are those two hundred verses.

Quit skirting the edge of the abyss. Tell yourself, "No more." You absolutely can stop the downward spiral. Address your fear. Don't shy away from it. Admit it. Cry out in prayer and tell God you are sinking, just like David did in Psalm 42:6, where he cried, "Oh, God, my soul is in despair within me; Therefore, I remember you."

God wants you physically, spiritually, and mentally healthy.

What's one thing you can do right now that will lighten your fear?

Can you voice Psalm 42:6 as a prayer? (*My soul is downcast; therefore I will remember you.*)

DAY 49

THAT GREEN-EYED MONSTER

> A tranquil heart give life to the flesh,
> but envy makes the bones rot.
> —Proverbs 14:30

Oh, that green-eyed monster. Like jealousy, he's not very pretty.

Why do we get jealous? Why do I get jealous?

I get jealous when I compare myself to others. As long as I'm content with my life, I seldom feel envious. Anytime I feel like I've come up short when compared to someone else, feelings of jealousy pop up. But we have to be willing to admit to our green-eyed monster if we're going to eliminate it.

We can express jealousy in many ways other than with words. Failure to express a compliment, ignoring someone, cutting someone out of the group or out of our lives, these are all ways we express our jealousy without ever opening our mouths.

Jealousy is as much about what we don't say or do as it is about what we do say and do.

But what about when you're the one other people are jealous of? If you've never been there, it might be hard to think someone is jealous of you, but I can almost guarantee someone has been jealous of you at some point in your life.

If you've knowingly experienced it, how did it make you feel? Someone once told me they thought I was born with a silver spoon in my mouth. That made me uncomfortable, and it also perturbed me a little. At that moment in my life, it might have looked that way because they hadn't seen all the years prior. They hadn't seen how hard I'd worked to attain even the smallest level of confidence.

When you feel jealous of someone, unless you know everything there is to know about that person, you might be wrong to envy them. You might be shortchanging them. To be jealous of someone often diminishes the hard work they've done to get to where they are.

Yes, some people are born wealthy, beautiful, and talented, but what possible good does it do us to be jealous about it?

Absolutely nothing.

There will always be those with more, but if you live in the United States, there are millions more around the world who have much, much less.

What makes us perfectly happy with our lives—and then whoosh, it's gone when we see something better? How do we go from being discontent with what we genuinely love to wanting something else? Surely we know there will always be someone with more. But why don't we also remember there's always someone with less?

I have a sign on a wall in my house that reads, "There is someone happy today with less than what you have." We need to remember that every day.

Keeping a gratitude journal is a great way to defuse jealousy. It's virtually impossible to be jealous if you're truly grateful.

I suggest a special little notebook just for this purpose. Or a happiness jar. I have a large jar on my countertop for that purpose. To be very honest, I'm not regular about dropping notes into it. But if days go by and I haven't written anything, it's a wake-up call.

Some people write in a gratitude journal every night before going to bed. If that works for you, that's great. I recently read an interesting article that stated it's more conducive to good sleep to write out a list of what you want to accomplish the next day instead of writing in a gratitude journal. It has more of a calming effect. In that case, you would write in your gratitude journal in the mornings.

The more you take note of your personal blessings, the less you will be jealous.

Dissatisfaction and even some jealousy can lead to good outcomes. If our jealousy prompts us to make the necessary changes to bring about personal fulfillment, it's a good thing. It's the rare person who makes significant changes in their lives without some form of discontent.

Get rid of the green-eyed monster. It does you no good, and it certainly feeds depression.

Is there someone you are jealous of?
Is it doing you any good?

DAY 50
WHOSE GUILT IS IT REALLY?

> Chronic remorse, as all the moralists are agreed, is a most undesirable sentiment.
> —Aldous Huxley

Some of us feel guilty about everything, as though we think we are responsible for the world. It's called false or chronic guilt, and the problem with false guilt is that at times it is a smokescreen for the real thing.

Sometimes, we almost want to feel guilty about things for which we are not guilty so we can ignore the areas where we are. For years, I took on the responsibility of the happiness of my loved ones and ignored other legitimate responsibilities I did have. When I couldn't make them happy—because who can?—I felt remorse. I didn't face areas of real guilt because I distracted myself with unnecessary guilt.

There are enough things we do every day that can provoke some real and, might I add, healthy feelings of guilt. We are responsible for the guilt that accompanies our own ill-advised decisions.

Real guilt can be a catalyst for healthy change.

False guilt almost never encourages healthy change. It can even get in the way of hearing God's voice in our lives because we are so busying doing our unnecessary *mea culpas,* we don't hear

His voice. We focus so much on our feelings of guilt that we're not much good for anything else.

I love 1 Corinthians 4:4, "I am conscious of nothing against myself, yet I am not acquitted, but the one who examines me is the LORD." I interpret this as Paul saying, "I am not aware of anything anyone has against me or accuses me of but that doesn't make me innocent, of course. But God will examine me." I like how Paul doesn't borrow any guilt that isn't rightly his.

False guilt can bring us down. People who are prone to depression often have a highly developed conscience. They are often very sensitive. When a friend or family member is sad or angry, they often think it's something they've said or done.

We need to admit when we are feeling guilty and then ask ourselves why. The feelings of guilt are a prompt for us to engage in self-examination. Why do we feel guilty so easily? What is in us that causes us to feel this way?

And, of course, other people try to put us on guilt trips. Because we are sensitive, we generally believe them. Don't allow anyone to place that burden on you.

Then there are other people who try to guilt us into doing things. When we are feeling guilty, we need to do two things:

- Accept real guilt but debunk false guilt.
- Ask yourself what you are feeling guilty about. If you can't come up with anything, it's probably nothing you said or did; it's your overdeveloped sense of responsibility.

Taking on responsibility that isn't ours can trigger depression because we don't have a clear understanding of what our responsibilities are and are not. We have been so conditioned to feel liable for everything, we just automatically put it all on ourselves.

Once you have a clear understanding of who and what you are responsible for, you are less likely to feel guilty about the things you are not responsible for. Refuse to let other people heap undeserved guilt on you.

Of course, our responsibilities, just like our lives, are ever changing. As our children grow, they assume more responsibility and ours diminish. But as our parents age, we may find ourselves once more responsible for others. Our responsibilities are as fluid as our lives are.

It is good to be a responsible person. But you do not have to fix everything and everyone, and you certainly don't need to allow undeserved, false guilt to weigh you down.

Do you find yourself feeling responsible for everyone?
Do you feel guilty when you think you have failed?

DAY 51
DISTRACTION IS A WONDERFUL THING

> Arise and do the next thing. If we are inspired of God, what is the next thing? To trust Him absolutely ... Never let the sense of failure corrupt your new action.
> —Oswald Chambers

The next thing is the same for everyone: trust God. That's always the first next step. Trust God for the next step you need to take. For many, the next step will need to be distraction because you are having a bad day with depression or anxiety—or just a bad day overall.

The great benefit of distraction is that the distractions can be simple. A therapist once told a patient (OK, it was me), "Distraction is a wonderful thing." It is.

It's nothing short of amazing how, if we can distract our minds with just one simple thing, it almost always leads to another simple thing. Then another. And so on. It gets us through the day.

But there is a time for this type of activity, and it's not all the time. Distractions are meant for those bad days. And it's important our *doing* isn't destructive or unhealthy. An unhealthy distraction always complicates depression, like overeating, oversleeping, and all the other *overs*.

A distraction is usually something mundane, routine, and ordinary. The simple act of tinkering in the garage or around the house, cleaning out a drawer, or organizing something gives us a sense of accomplishment and, most importantly, relief from our crowded, chaotic, and confused mind.

Some days, we have no strength to do the hard work of fighting our depression or searching for the reasons. We just need to get through the day. Those are the days that instead of working hard to get better, we just *are*.

Doing the next thing works for us when we feel anxious as well. That's when we really need to divert our thoughts. If you start to do anything at all, your mind detours away from your thoughts because you're focusing on something else. Very often, the anxious thoughts subside for a while, sometimes for good.

This kind of approach is nothing new. We distract ourselves by looking away when we are given an injection so as not to feel anxious. We focus on something else when we're in physical pain. When we watch a scary movie, we hide our face in our hands when it becomes too frightening for us. It's a natural response to fear and anxiety.

We can handle a lot of things by focusing our attention elsewhere. It seems to me that in Philippians 4:6, the apostle Paul is showing us how distraction can work. When we are anxious, he tells us to distract ourselves by giving thanks—a true thought distractor if I ever heard one.

He goes even further by telling us what thoughts serve as distractors: true thoughts; noble thoughts; right, pure, lovely, admirable, excellent, and praiseworthy thoughts. This pattern works great for diverting our negative thinking. It's not always possible to simply quit thinking negative thoughts. Replacing or diverting them is usually better.

But then we might need other distractions as well. Jesus distracted the disciples during the storm by walking on the water and causing their attention to focus on Him and not the storm. Of course, we know that Peter was negatively distracted when he tried to actually walk on water and instead looked at the waves and started to sink. There is obviously a wrong time to be distracted! But Peter did walk on the water, so there is that.

We have to be intentional about distracting ourselves when we are feeling depressed or anxious. It's a good idea to have a list of things on hand we can pick from before our moods plummet or we feel anxious. If we have activities to choose from in advance, we will find relief even sooner. Anxiety responds particularly well to this type of action therapy if used at the very first symptom.

Remember when I said depression responds to very simple interventions? It really does. Distracting ourselves is one of those simple steps that seems almost too simple. But give it a try. You will be surprised how this simple act helps.

Do you need a respite today from your mind?
Is there something you can get up and do right now? Anything?

DAY 52

WHAT DO YOUR WORDS SAY ABOUT YOU?

> But the things that come out of a person's mouth
> come from the heart, and these defile them.
> —Matthew 15:18

Your feelings, and consequently your actions, all start in your mind. If we all really believed this, our lives would change dramatically. The world would change dramatically as well.

Try to get mad without thinking mad thoughts. You can't. The next time you are mad, try getting over being mad without changing your angry thoughts. You can't.

Let's look at some examples where thoughts resulted in disastrous outcomes and examples of those that didn't. In all these cases, people thought before they spoke or acted.

Eve thought about eating the fruit before she ate it. Cain thought about killing his brother before he did so. Moses thought about hitting the rock before he actually hit it. David thought about killing Uzziah before he made the actual plan. Jonah thought about rebelling before he rebelled. Peter thought about denying before he denied. Ananias and Sapphira thought about lying before they lied. These thoughts all resulted in disastrous outcomes. Here's the flipside.

Esther thought about how to approach the king before she approached him. Ruth thought about her plan before she spoke to her mother-in-law. Daniel thought about his actions before he defied the king. These thoughts resulted in positive outcomes.

Words begin as thoughts, then turn into either words or actions or even both.

Sad to say, but our words reflect who we are. When I first realized what my words said about me, I was appalled and ashamed. I had only to listen to my words to know where my heart was.

Harsh, mean, condemning words don't come from a loving, kind, forgiving heart. That's hard to hear and even harder to admit. But it's true. Instinctively, we all know it's true. But the good news is we can actually trick our mind. Here's an experiment to try.

For one day, change your words to positive, mood-lifting, encouraging words spoken to yourself and others. How did you feel at the end of the day? I think I know. Outside of it feeling a little disingenuous, you felt much better. In addition, you made others feel better too.

When we speak life-affirming words, we hear the words we are using, and our mind follows suit. But to make lasting change, we have to begin with our heart.

It's amazing how our moods and the moods of others are influenced by something as simple as our words. It is not true that sticks and stones can break my bones, but words will never hurt me. We can recover and forget about broken bones. We almost never forget harmful, hateful words.

As the third chapter of James states, the tongue is a restless evil full of deadly poison. That's pretty serious. James goes further to say we humans can't tame our tongues. And that's true as well. We can't. By ourselves that is. With God's help, we can.

Think of it like this. Our words are like a bicycle chain that connects our heart to our mouth. Our words (the wheels) are driven by what preoccupies our heart (the chain.) So, we have to deal with the chain first to drive our words where they should go. Our heart is where our emotions and our thoughts live. So, our heart has to be right. And there's no quicker way to know where our heart is than by listening to what comes out of our mouths. It can be downright humiliating!

Even now, I continue to listen to myself after years of doing this because it's such a barometer of my heart health. For all my good behavior, my words still remain a dead giveaway as to what is going on inside. Actively listening to ourselves is the first step in "keeping our thoughts captured." As an added bonus, it will help us manage our moods and depression better.

Have you ever really listened to the words you speak?
Will you actively do that today?

DAY 53

THINK ABOUT WHAT YOU ARE THINKING ABOUT

> Think about the true, the honorable, the right,
> the pure, the lovely, and the good.
> —My paraphrase of Philippians 4:8

Thinking about what you are thinking about sounds like an oxymoron. But it works. Schedule some times throughout your day to examine how you've been thinking. It's really quite easy once you get the hang of it. Use your feelings and words as a barometer.

Dr. Caroline Leaf says this in her book, *Switch on Your Brain*: "As we think, we change the physical nature of our brain. As we consciously direct our thinking, we can wire out toxic patterns of thinking and replace them with healthy thoughts."

For example, if you are feeling fear, have you been thinking anxious thoughts? If your stomach is upset, have you been thinking stressful thoughts? Remember, science has proven beyond any doubt that the connection and the reaction between our mind and body are inextricably linked.

Track your mood on a particular day. If you're feeling happy and contented, it is highly likely you have been thinking positive, constructive thoughts. If you're feeling angry, discouraged, sad, etc., you've probably been doing some negative thinking.

If you find recognizing your thoughts too difficult at first, look at your words. What words have been coming out of your mouth? If you've been using words like *angry, mad, upset,* and *frustrated,* you've probably talked yourself right into a bad mood. To repeat, words are the result of thoughts.

There are also trigger words/thoughts we speak to ourselves, "I should" being one of them. "I should" can be a very destructive phrase. "I should" do this or that, "I should get a different job," "I should …" Saying "I should" often leads to shame. It's so much better to say, "Maybe I could do this or that." "Perhaps, there is another alternative." "Maybe I need to pray about it more."

"I wish" is another one. I wish I were prettier, smarter, more talented. I wish I had more money. There is certainly nothing wrong with wishing, but if that's all we're doing, and we're not taking steps to make some of those wishes come true, we're just thinking in circles.

We can take time throughout the day to make a few quick notes on paper or on our phone, or even mental notes, tuck them away, get on with our day, and then later talk to God about them.

Our thought life is the catalyst for how our day is going to go. If we don't harness our thoughts before we speak them or act on them, we can do a lot of damage to ourselves and others. When we say, "I just wasn't thinking," in essence, what we are saying is "I wasn't aware of what I was thinking."

Of course, it's impossible to be totally aware of our thoughts every minute. But it is possible to be aware of our thoughts much of the time, especially if our thoughts are focused on God. Thoughts lead to word choice, and word choice is important no matter to whom the words are directed.

It's important to use kinder words with ourselves as well. For example, let's say we make a mistake at work, leave something out of a recipe (me), or we forget to get gas and find ourselves stuck on the side of the road. None of these mean we are a terrible person. It simply means we made a mistake, so don't use words that suggest anything else. Keep the words directed at yourself as gentle as they would be for someone else.

There are some people who would never speak an unkind word to another person, but they constantly berate themselves. Depressed people often speak harsher to themselves than they would to anyone else.

Words once spoken are always remembered by the author and the receiver, especially when they are the same person.

How have you been thinking today?
Do you even know?

DAY 54

YOU'VE GOT TO "MOVE IT, MOVE IT, MOVE IT"

> Move it or lose it.
> —From a TV commercial

Physical movement has become almost a spiritual discipline for me. I have literally walked off many an anxiety attack. Exercise has been proven to be as effective as medication if done regularly. A twenty-minute walk five days a week is enough to get you started. The research is overwhelming as to the benefit of exercise for mental health. Some mental health experts even suggest that exercise is as effective as antidepressants.

I know how hard this might be for some of you. It's very, very hard to even think of walking for twenty minutes when all you want to do is stay in bed.

The mind over matter approach is awfully hard when the matter IS the mind.

But if you want to get better, this suggestion is one of the best. If I could be right beside you, spurring you on and panting with you, I would. But I am there in spirit.

Even your posture can make a difference. Walk with your head up, your shoulders back, and with a confident stride. Believe it or not, postures such as hanging our heads or stooping over perpetuate feelings of depression. But when we keep our heads up, our shoulders back, and walk briskly and confidently, our mind is fooled into thinking we really are OK. It actually changes our own perception of ourselves. Try it.

Exercise, however, does not cancel the need for rest. Depression is energy depleting. Sometimes rest and relaxation is exactly what you need. As long as our rest periods are intentional and brief (meaning we have purposely decided to rest, depression didn't decide for us), they are helpful.

The reason intentionality is so important is because depression likes nothing more than to keep us down, literally as well as physically. If you decide to take some time for yourself, you will feel empowered because *you* made that decision. Just watch out that you don't sit for so long people can identify your spot on the sofa by the identifiable print.

I wish you could have been on my journey with me when I started to routinely walk. First of all, I had to make myself do it. Secondly, the weather conditions had to be just so. No cloudy days, no windy days, no too-hot days, and especially no really cold days.

Now, I've walked on days so cold I'm bundled up to the point that only my eyes are uncovered. I walk on snowy days, even misty days. On hot and humid days, I walk early or use my treadmill. In other words, I walk no matter what. No excuses.

Smiling is another moving tool that bears repeating. Did you know the physical act of smiling has scientifically been proven to release good-feeling hormones into your body? It signals the mind that you are not depressed. Smile when you answer the phone. Smile at the checkout girl, the waitress, and so on. Get the picture?

Another "move it" example. Make yourself smile no matter how disingenuous it feels. Don't forget, *acting as if* is a legitimate therapy. It isn't hypocritical, and here's why.

It's a behavior not meant to fool anyone but yourself. It's a behavior you use to get yourself out of a slump. It works. When you smile, other people smile back, and it makes you realize the world might not be such a bad place after all. Remember, that person you smile at may be having a bad day too. Walking around with our heads down, looking glum, is not going to elicit any positive encounters with people, and positive encounters improve our moods.

If you're wondering if it's possible to smile when you feel really depressed, it is. Trust me, it won't seem genuine at all. That's not the point. The point is to get those signals to your brain.

And, of course, if you do force a smile, more than likely someone will smile back, and that's a win-win.

Can you "move it, move it, move it"?
Will you try to smile more often?

DAY 55

THE SCOURGE OF MINDLESS SITTING

*Mindless sitting does nothing more than
make a giant dent in the seat cushion.*

I purposefully left this subject until close to the end because so many people have a hard time believing physical activity can help depression. Also, we are getting ready to open the toolbox, and physical activity is mentioned more than once in the different compartments. You need to know and remember this next statement.

Mindless sitting is a breeding ground for depression.

The depressed mind, highly influenced by the body and left unfocused for very long, will sink to its lowest common denominator, and that is inertness. We become content to sit and sit and sit. Moving then becomes a herculean effort. Sitting becomes a habit, a really bad one for our overall health.

But when we move, a number of good things take place in our body.

- Our blood circulation improves.
- We breathe better because we are upright.
- Physical movement activates our good hormones, and we get a little mental boost as well.
- Anxiety decreases.

- We lose weight.
- Cancer rates goes down, and many other good health things happen.

Activity of any kind often prompts other activity, and pretty soon our minds are distracted. And as you now know, distraction is a wonderful thing. Some days, this has been my mantra, and I've repeated it over and over. But to get distracted, one generally has to move. I've never known a depressed person who has not felt better with the simple activity of physical movement.

A study from the Mayo Clinic, https://www.mayoclinic.org/healthy-lifestyle/adult-health/expert-answers/sitting/faq-20058005, suggests we should move every thirty minutes.

How we move is also important. Believe it or not, there is some validity to moving slower than usual if anxiety is a big part of your depression. Very often, when we are anxious, we find ourselves moving and talking too fast.

And even when we are not anxious, fast moving and talking can make us feel like we are anxious, like the effects of too much caffeine. When we are dashing from one thing to another, our minds might read that as anxiety, and the body will correspondingly respond with fast breathing and hyperventilation.

The body responds the same to real *or* perceived anxiety just like it does to real or perceived danger. It doesn't know the difference between the real and the unreal, so shortness of breath, for example, might well be interpreted by our mind as anxiety. I wish I had time to go into this more deeply. It's eye-opening.

When our bodies react with a fight-or-flight response in a dangerous situation, that's a good thing. But when our bodies are in a constant fight-or-flight stance, it's counter-productive. Excess cortisol gets dumped in our bodies and causes physical damage. Our bodies were never meant to stay in a hypervigilant state.

Anxiety was a major component of my depression, and I found that on my most anxious days, I consciously made myself talk slower and walk slower. This approach works when anxiety is feeding your hyperactivity. I still monitor myself and adjust my movements as needed.

If sluggishness is the problem, do just the opposite. Walk faster and more energetic. After a while, this all becomes automatic. I don't even think about it anymore. I automatically speed up or slow down, depending on whether I'm sluggish or anxious. This little mind-tricking exercise really works.

We need to move, and we need to move in a way that contributes to our overall mental health.

Do you understand the connection between depression and physical movement?

Will you observe yourself for this connection?

DAY 56
A SURPRISE ATTACK

> Do not be afraid of sudden fear ... for the Lord ...
> will keep your foot from being caught.
> —Proverbs 3:25

I was in the final writing of this book when I woke up in the early morning hours, June 3, 2020, to be exact, and couldn't believe the heavy feelings that were weighing on me. I recognized them all too well, but it had been at least twenty years since I felt this overwhelming, sudden anxiety.

Yes, there was a serious worldwide pandemic, but I knew that wasn't the trigger. I questioned whether to share this and decided I would because sometimes a picture is worth a thousand words.

Below is my word picture describing how I felt.

> I see the dark shadow in the corner, and I am afraid. Surely it isn't *it* after all these years. I am so scared; I think I'm not even breathing.
>
> But *it* pounces from the corner, and I stand transfixed, not knowing where to run. I feel *it* nipping at my body.

It feels like the thing is trying to eat me a piece at a time. It hurts. My breathing gets heavier as I feel the pressure in my chest that is almost more than I can bear.

I feel hopeless, helpless. I feel overburdened by the writing. I feel disconnected and alone. Mostly, I'm as frightened as I've ever been.

As *it* continues to bite, I am so taken aback by this sudden attack. I can't move. It's almost as if I've decided to let *it* have its way and just consume me. I am transfixed. But then something happens.

Call it the Holy Spirit, the voice of God, my own survival instinct, but I begin to think of a young David holding slingshot, facing his giant. I have more than a slingshot. I have God's word; the power of the Holy Spirit and I have my toolbox.

I have everything I need to fight this battle. I remember 2 Peter 2:3, "His power has granted to us everything pertaining to life and godliness."

I gather my spiritual weapons, and I stand up, tall and fierce. No giant is going to take me down. Not ever again.

First, I whack at this thing trying to eat me. I send him sailing across the room. He springs back in attack.

He keeps attacking and I keep fighting, using this weapon or that. Finally, *it* realizes I'm not going to quit. *It* retreats to its corner in defeat.

I am tired from the battle. I curl up under God's wings and rest there as long as I need to. It feels so soft and warm and cushy; I don't ever want leave. This is my safe place. It's good to feel protected.

But eventually I have to leave. There is a life to live, a book to finish, and I'm so praying it will help others fight their own battles with depression.

I leave my nest, emboldened by what God has whispered to me. I can do this. I pick up my slingshot and I dare *it* to come out of hiding.

"You are nothing but a coward!" I yell. "Come out, come out wherever you are," I taunt, but *it* stays silent, cowering in fear.

Do you recall what I wrote in the introduction about how sometimes we won't know what triggers an episode? Well, this was one of those times. I knew it wasn't depression. I knew it was anxiety because anxiety is a sudden attack.

There was no identifiable reason anxiety should have attacked like that unless Satan was working overtime to stop this book from being written. Don't underestimate Satan's desire to destroy our faith. Sometimes Satan sends anxious feelings our way, especially when we are attempting something for God.

I was fine by the end of the day. That also proved it was an anxiety attack and not depression.

The tools I used are the very ones I am about to introduce you to. As someone in an online writing group I belong to told me, there is only one being that would prefer for this book to not get published, and he is like a fierce, roaring lion (1 Peter 5:8).

I am "standing firm in my faith."

That's what you have to do. Stand firm and tall. Fight your way out of an anxiety attack when fighting is the right approach. Don't attack anxiety with a feather but with the sword of the Spirit that demolishes strongholds. Equip yourself with the Word of God and prayer.

Anxiety attacks can be quelled.

Does my word picture sound like something you've experienced?

Will you stand firm in your faith?

DAY 57

DAVID, GOLIATH, AND DEPRESSION

> You come against me with sword and spear and javelin, but I come against you in the of the Lord Almighty ... This day the Lord will deliver.
> —1 Samuel 17:45

Sometimes depression feels like Goliath, and we feel like a young boy with only a slingshot.

Do you know why David refused to wear the suggested armor? Why in the world would he choose what seemed to be such an ineffective weapon, a slingshot?

For one thing, he knew how to use a slingshot. He knew nothing about using heavy armor, and it would've only weighed him down anyway.

In Malcolm Gladwell's book *David and Goliath*, he writes that Goliath might well have had acromegaly, which accounted for his body size. People with acromegaly also have poor eyesight. Goliath wouldn't see a small stone coming his way, while he might well see a shiny spear or at least its reflection. Plus, a stone well placed in the middle of the forehead is fatal.

Like David, we all face our Goliaths. And depression is an awfully big giant. I think we forget, however, that just like David, we can fight and win the battle against our own giant.

David didn't have any special tools except for one, his belief that God would give him the victory. We, too, might only have a slingshot, but a slingshot is all we need if God is the force that powers that slingshot.

I have faced my Goliath a few times. And sometimes I thought I needed some fancy weapons, but inevitably, I always came back to prayer, God's Word, and my toolbox.

I am not suggesting that by only praying and studying our Bibles, we can easily defeat our personal giant. I am also *not* suggesting that prayer and Bible study alone couldn't bring swift victory if God so chooses. But we still have to learn how to use our tools like David learned his slingshot skills, because practice breeds confidence.

You never know when a giant might just show up.

We, too, learn our skills by practicing. It took time to learn how prayer and Bible study worked for me in battling depression. I had to learn to study my Bible and not read it devotionally only. I had to memorize verses so I would have them immediately at my disposal.

I also had to learn to pray honestly without pretending I was holier than I was. It took me a long time to put aside all I had heard about prayer and all the prayers I heard. I had the impression that they were supposed to be stilted and formal. Oh, and long.

It wasn't until I read most of the prayers in the Bible that I realized that prayer never has to be long for long's sake. The longest prayer in the Bible is called Ezra's prayer (Ezra 9–10 and Nehemiah 1–2), and it can be prayed in under fifteen minutes.

Then I paid attention to the *how* of those prayers. I was struck by two things: the honest emotions living comfortably with a reverence for God.

When it came to Bible study, I realized the Bible was the most interesting book I had ever read. It was alive and living and a two-edged sword (Hebrews 4:12). It offers hope while at the same time opening our eyes to our innermost flaws, the hidden ones we don't even know about it.

God is the force behind my slingshot. My stones are the basic spiritual disciplines of Bible study, prayer, fasting, tithing, silence, and solitude.

That's how I fight my Goliath.

How do you fight your Goliath? Your Goliath might be different from mine, but we all have access to the same slingshot and stones.

When you feel small and ill equipped, remember you serve the same God that a young shepherd boy did. If God helped him win his battle, there's every reason to believe He will help you win yours.

How are you fighting your giant?
What tools are you using?

DAY 58
THE BEST SELF-HELP BOOK

Study to show yourself.
—2 Timothy 2:15

Hundreds of books have been written about Bible study, and you can find lots of various study methods online. But for now, let's tackle the two most quoted reasons for not studying God's Word.

It's too hard.

Well, let me ask you this. Do you read other things? Do you read other books? Do you read how-to manuals? Saying the Bible is too hard to understand is an excuse—a flimsy one at that.

Yes, some parts are hard to understand. Not just hard to understand in a literary sense, because the language is stilted at times and names impossible to pronounce, but the Bible is also hard to understand just because it confounds us.

It confuses us.

It challenges us. ("You expect me to do what, Lord?")

But I'm not suggesting you read the entire Bible all at once. It's a big book. There are lots of daily reading plans that will get you through it in a year. The more you read, the more everything just starts to fall into place.

I'm just suggesting you read it. It is God's Word revealed to us. It addresses every human condition. It provides guidance for every circumstance we will ever face. It addresses our emotions, from joy to despair. It offers grace and mercy and relief from our emotional pain.

God will meet you in His Word, and while perhaps difficult in the beginning, the more you read, the more things become clear. Why would it be otherwise? This is His book, about Him. He wants you to know everything about Him that you can know.

I started off like most people, thinking that the Old Testament was practically barbaric. When I got to the New Testament, I thought I could breathe a sigh of relief. But then Jesus took the law and made it even harder by making it more personal. In addition to loving God, now I am to love my neighbor as myself? And here I was expecting to read only warm and fuzzy verses that tell me Jesus loves me. Some people get stuck here because they are happy with pablum.

But while Jesus does love us, Jesus is also holy. Don't ever forget that. Jesus was sometimes tough on those He loved.

Furthermore, the Bible is the first place we should go for wisdom. It's the first place we should go for comfort.

"I don't have time."

Life is pretty hectic these days for everyone. Our days are so crowded we feel we can't possibly squeeze anything else into our fleeting twenty-four hours. And let's face it: depending on our season and our responsibilities, some of us have more discretionary times than others.

At the same time, as we all know, we can usually find time somewhere (even if it's the bathroom) to take a few minutes to read. Don't use time constraints as an excuse to avoid reading. Besides, those who study the Bible most are probably also the busiest.

The Bible has so much to say about depression and anxiety. There is no self-help book out there with as much to offer. It is in your best interest to read it. God wrote it for that purpose. He wrote because He knew we would need it. It's His second-best gift to us.

DEPRESSION HAS A BIG VOICE

I know this for sure. If you open your Bible, God will speak to you through His Word. He will give you the words to encourage you. There isn't another piece of literature that can equip us as well for the struggle with depression.

When was the last time you read your Bible?
What is holding you back?

DAY 59

PRAYER: EASIER THAN YOU THINK

> Any concern too small to be turned into a prayer
> is too small to be made into a burden.
> —Corrie Ten Boom

I am not suggesting that if we pray, our depression will vanish. I'm not saying it won't either. There have been times when I've prayed, and my mood lightened immediately. There have been other times I've prayed, and my depression remained, but at least I felt empowered to wade through it. As I said on day fifty-seven, I relearned a lot about prayer.

Prayer is a learning experience, for sure.

This devotional for today isn't about how to pray as much as it is about the importance of prayer in battling depression. I still read more books about prayer than any other subject. It wasn't always that way. For a long time, my focus was on depression, and my library card and personal library reflected that.

In my research, I came across the writing of the ancients, meaning those books written by monks and priests many years ago. They were eye-opening. These men and women seemed to have a better understanding of the majesty, sanctity, and privilege of prayer. When you are doing better, give them a try and read some books by the Desert Priests, along with the greats like Thomas a'Kempis, Charles Spurgeon, Henry Nouwen, C. S.

Lewis, Richard Foster, Oswald Chambers, and E.M. Bounds. They are challenging, but the results are well worth the journey.

There is a place for modern authors as well. Dallas Willard, Andy Stanley, John Ortberg, Beth Moore, and Phillip Yancey are some of my favorites.

Watch out for the cutesy stuff. Don't get your knowledge from the inside of a candy wrapper. Reading trustworthy Christian literature or reading a bunch of trite memes posted to social media is the difference between reading a Harlequin romance and a Leo Tolstoy novel. (No insult intended here.) There is a lot of inaccurate and make-you-feel-good literature on the market. Avoid those.

My personal prayer life has changed dramatically. While I remain an avid proponent of carving out time each day for prayer, I no longer feel chagrined or sinful should the day get beyond me through no fault of my own. If you are a caregiver for an ill person, or have very young children and work outside the home, or other such circumstances, you know what I mean.

Some days, I'm more of an archer, shooting up prayers as needed. Not the best choice, but we can be honest and admit that somedays it's the only choice. And there are days when our actions *are* our prayers. Some prayers are spoken through service to others.

But most times, I guard that time of day as though it's a precious jewel that could slip off my finger if I'm not careful. I've learned that my prayer life doesn't always look the same day after day. While God remains ever constant, my prayer life is ever evolving. I encourage you to develop the spiritual discipline of establishing a regular prayer time. Let it develop naturally.

As far as a physical position, we can kneel, sit, stand, or lie prostrate on the floor. Praying in bed is OK if it's a quick prayer before sleep or an early-morning prayer before we get up. Some people pray the same prayer every day before they hop out of bed.

We can pray with our eyes open or closed, silently or out loud. While praying in the car might be necessary in an emergency, it is not the place you should habitually use for your prayer time. It, too, qualifies as distracted driving.

I pray out loud. Often, I start praying, and then it's like God sets up a detour, and I find myself praying in a completely different manner. I find myself interceding with requests for people that seem to be coming out of someone else's mouth. Sometimes, I've even asked out loud, "Where did that come from, Lord?"

When that happens, I feel as though I've learned more about how God works because the Holy Spirit is interceding and supplying me with words that are in agreement with God's will for me and others in my life. I am "joining God in what He is already doing," as Henry Blackabee writes in *Experiencing God*.

When we hear our own words, it's not nearly as hard to determine whether our prayer is shallow or selfish. It doesn't take long to hear the insincerity, the whining, the constant me, me, me.

Does prayer seem elusive at times?
Are you satisfied with your prayer life?

DAY 60
UNPACK YOUR SUITCASE

> When I was a child, I spoke like a child, I thought like a child, I reasoned like a child. When I became a man, I gave up childish ways.
> —1 Corinthians 13:11

Boy, this is hard.

Unpacking our suitcase means looking at our mess. We all have a messy suitcase.

Generally, it's packed with bad memories, family disputes, hurt feelings, anger, bitterness, and much more. It could be packed with trauma or physical or emotional abuse. It could be packed with illness or disability. Most of our suitcases are so heavy we can't lift them.

Until we can.

That means, once we open them, examine the contents, get rid of most them, and make amends to and for what we can't dispose of (like people), we can lighten the load.

But the thing about your suitcase?

It's your suitcase we're talking about. It's your baggage. No one else's. You can't empty anyone's suitcase but your own. And no one can do it for you either. We can talk to a therapist, a pastor, or a friend. They can listen and help, but they can't unpack for us.

And it doesn't matter who packed it in the first place; it's up to you to unpack it. That sounds seriously unfair, and you know what? It is. But that doesn't change the fact that only you can ditch your baggage.

I had a lot of junk in my suitcase that I never put there. In fact, most of it. Over the years, I certainly added my own though. There was a time I used that as an excuse for my depression, but I eventually realized that I couldn't possibly hold anything against those who filled my suitcase with garbage. Why?

Because Christ had forgiven me, I had no choice but to forgive them.

Every time we shift responsibility for our troubles to other people, and yes, our moods, we take another step away from healing. Unpacking our suitcase means putting away the childish behavior that says, "It's not my fault."

We've all read about runners who run marathons with artificial legs, swimmers who swim with no arms, people who become millionaires though having been born in poverty. We try to convince ourselves they have a special inner strength that we don't. But do you know the source of their strength?

Their strength came because they unpacked their suitcases and chose not to carry around their disabilities as an excuse.

People who grow in Christ are people who know that despite what's in their suitcase, they have a choice. They can keep carrying their baggage around, or they can dump it out.

But how?

Ask some questions.

What are the items you can throw away because they don't serve you well anymore, like bitterness, jealousy, and anger, for example? How about those memories of abuse? What are they doing for you? How is any of this getting you to where you want to be? Throw them in the garbage. There is no need to carry them around any longer.

But what about the things you are responsible for? Like the blowup you had with someone so long ago you don't even remember what it was about. The person you might have borrowed money from but never repaid. Fill in the blanks.

Those can't be thrown away until they are dealt with. How that happens will depend on many things, but you at least have to try. If you don't, you might as well put them back in your suitcase and carry them around the rest of your life.

This all sounds harsh. But do you know who are the strongest advocates of this approach?–The very people who have suffered more than they needed to because they almost didn't empty their suitcase.

Like me.

I knew I had to empty my suitcase and throw away a lot of the things from the past if I didn't want to continue to experience episodes of depression. In that process, my toolbox was created. I knew I needed tools I could rely on every time depression/anxiety or low mood reared their heads. The toolbox includes all the tools I used then and still use today to manage my moods.

Have you ever built anything? Have you ever started any kind of a project? What's the first thing you did? Well, the first thing you are supposed to do is get your tools all lined up. Right?

Let's use a recipe, for example. The tools to cook something might be a pan, some utensils, some herbs or spices, some sort of cooking medium like oil or butter, and of course a stove. Without these, you aren't going to get very far.

How about painting something, whether a wall or a picture? You need the paint, the drop cloth, the brushes, a cleaning agent, some rags, and so on.

In both cases, the tools are essential for a good outcome. So, let's open the toolbox and begin to get better.

PART TWO
THE TOOLBOX

INTRODUCTION TO THE TOOLBOX

This toolbox is yours. You can take out the tools that don't work for you and add some that do. But a word of caution before throwing away a tool: try it out first. You might even decide to rearrange them.

There's a good chance you will pick up one and think it seems too silly and too simple. But until you try it, how will you know? Like smiling when you answer the phone. It almost seems an insult to suggest that when we are really feeling depressed, we can even muster up a smile, much less smile when we answer the phone. But if you do it, after a while you will start to notice a difference. (Remember, it's merely forcing the corners of your mouth to go up.)

While some tools are going to sound too easy, some will seem like too much work, like exercising. First of all, I'm using the word loosely; it can just be a simple twenty-minute walk. But even that might sound like too much of an effort. If you want to get better though, some of this *is* going to be hard.

In my view, what's harder? Talking a twenty-minute walk or feeling depressed the rest of your life? For me, it was no contest.

And while I've used the word *simple* often when referring to the tools, simple doesn't necessarily mean easy. So, don't confuse the two, and don't try to implement all of them all at once.

You might wonder why there are no specific tools listed for something I've written about. They are there, but they might not directly reference a certain day's subject. But I've painstakingly reread every page and made sure there was a tool in the toolbox that works for that particular issue.

Many of the tools focus on feelings and will suggest you accurately acknowledge those feelings. This is so important. It does absolutely no good to pretend you're feeling something other than what you are feeling. God knows it anyway. He can handle every emotion you have, but dishonesty will create a barrier only you can remove.

And in case you think God couldn't possibly understand your human emotions, read this from Ezekiel: 6:9, *"Those who escape will remember Me ... how I have been hurt by their adulterous hearts which turned away from me."* That is the God of the universe saying He's hurt. Do you need any more proof?

I have listed in the appendices a number of ways for you to distract yourself as a kind of prompting, something that might spark an interest. There are many internet sites that will give you more ideas. Search under words such as "hobbies" or "sports" or "distraction activities"

Many of these tools will be found in every compartment. I don't include Bible study and prayer because I consider them nonoptional. Please remember that.

There is an abundance of tools in some compartments, especially the everyday tools. Don't let the number overwhelm you. They are for you to pick from as needed.

For your first day, you might want to single out just a few and try them on. You might not want to even start with the everyday tools. That's OK.

It's your toolbox.

Also, you will find many of the same tools in different compartments. That's because many of them overlap. Walking and distraction, for example, work for every symptom.

Finally, this all takes time. Don't think you will master these tools in one day. You won't. I certainly didn't. And to think this will be easy is an affront to all those people, myself included, who have worked really hard to get better.

Malcom Gladwell, in his book *The Outliers*, has researched how long it takes the average person to become a master at a skill for which a person has some innate ability. (I could practice the violin for forever and never be a concert violinist.) Anyway, it takes ten thousand hours. But that's not the only point Gladwell was making. The point he is making is learning anything requires time and hard work. There's just no way around it. And this is most certainly a learning process.

You will be learning what works for you and what doesn't. You will be learning new ways to think and behave.

When I was working on this book, I found the writing easy. But all the technical stuff was overwhelming. I almost threw my hands up and quit for good. I came to the end of my learning curve time and again. But I would walk away for whatever time I needed and come back with a fresh enthusiasm. Let me say clearly:

There will be days in your recovery process where picking up any tool will prove way too heavy. Do not chastise yourself. This is the day you simply put one foot in front of the other. The heaviness is probably making you feel like your feet have been poured in concrete.

On those days, squeeze God's hand as much as you need to. He will not let go, and He will not let you fall over from the weight. He will help you lift one foot after the other.

I love what Dr. Cloud and Dr. Townsend wrote in *God Will Make a Way*: "God heals the most when we are injured the most."

But God also loves the most when we feel the most unloved.

Be kind to yourself on these days. Let the toolbox sit. But don't continue to let it sit. With severe cases of depression, you may need more than the toolbox. Get the help you need.

I was sitting on my deck today starting to feel just a little discouraged about this book, the first time in a long time. Who is going to read it? No. That's not quite accurate. Is *anybody* going to read it? I don't have a platform, except for my small blog, so who is even going to know it exists? (Hopefully, you recognize my faulty and negative thinking.)

I thought about what I've been writing. I thought about all the ideas I'm giving you, the tools to help you overcome your depression, and I got up, fixed some hot tea, came inside, and sat down in front of this computer.

As you can see, I used two of my own tools, movement and distraction. I use these two tools the most consistently.

I finally concluded that even if I am never aware of anyone outside family and friends (who I will forcibly make read this book), it will be out there in the universe.

I just thought of something exciting. This book will live on till the end of time. Wow! I hadn't thought about that.

People a hundred years from now might go to a garage sale, assuming they are still a thing, and find a dusty book written by yours truly. They will thumb through it because it has a great cover and title, and they might say, "Hey, this looks really good."

"How much is it?" they might ask.

"It's free," the lady in the garage says.

Oh, well.

Moving on:

I remembered that just the other day, I found a really old book at Goodwill. It's called the *Go-Getter*. It's a short funny little book by an unknown author, at least to me. It's written in stilted language and uses phrases I've never even heard. I read it in under an hour. It was a charming book and had a great message about perseverance. I know. Right? God's timing.

Well, my book might end up dusty and forgotten by the world, but that's really OK. I mean that. I know I will meet my Savior someday, and when He asks me if I wrote the book He told me to write (of course, He already knows; the question is for my benefit), I will jump up and down and yell, "Yes! Yes, I did." (I get weepy every time I read this.)

I persevered. I did what I knew to do, and God stepped in and did the rest. He will do the same for you. Praise His name. So, here's the toolbox.

THE EVERYDAY TOOLS

- **Get up. Make up the bed. Shut the door.** All of these make a huge impact on your day. Shutting the door means shutting the door to the possibility of going back to bed. While a nap later on may be OK, don't nap in bed. Too much of a danger you will stay there.
- **Make yourself presentable.** When you look in the mirror, you want to see a person *you* would like to know.
- **Have your time with God through Bible study and prayer.** I can't start my day unless I've made that connection with God. If you don't believe in God, then just take some time to reflect.
- **Exercise.** Walk, bike, it doesn't matter what, but do it at least five days a week for at least twenty minutes. If there is one guarantee I can make, it's that this will help your mood.
- **Maintain a regular sleeping and waking pattern.** Do this even on weekends.
- **Connect with people.** Reach out to someone at least a couple of times a week. Phone calls and in person are best, but even texting and social media are good for now.
- **Practice deep breathing a few times a day.** If anxiety is a big part of your depression, this really helps. The best book on this subject is Herbert Benson's *The Relaxation Response*. This will book will teach you how to breathe properly and can immediately reduce anxiety.

- **Eat healthily.** Eat more veggies and fruits and fewer carbs. Watch the sugar. (This is my problem area.) Sugar can be a huge problem for some people because of the extreme swings in blood sugar levels. Swinging is for monkeys, not people.
- **Limit caffeine if it is a problem.** Too much caffeine can make some people think they're having an anxiety attack even when they're not. Your mind doesn't know the difference.
- **Get up and move every hour** or so. (Thirty minutes is even better.)
- **Smile when you answer the phone.** Push up the corners of your mouth. Remember, it releases good endorphins, and you will feel better.
- **Build margin into your life.** Take stock of how much time you spend daily doing certain activities. Is there a way to streamline things? Don't let Satan steal your time.
- **Take stock of your habits.** What are you doing habitually that is not helpful? What are you not doing that should become a new habit? What are you doing that doesn't need doing?
- **Minimize stress by minimizing the drama.** If it isn't your drama and you have no responsibility for it, remember, it's not your circus, and it's not your monkeys.
- **Prepare yourself for sleep.** Schedule your bedtime and make sure everything you need to do for tomorrow is done so you can fall asleep without worrying.
- **Have a plan for days when you aren't feeling well.**

The Words and Thoughts Tools

- **Use life-affirming words when speaking to others and especially to yourself.** God wants you healthy and whole, so speak hopeful and encouraging words to

yourself and others. When you hear your own words, you will feel uplifted.
- **Stay alert to the words that are popping into your head throughout your day.** Examine them later. How were your words and moods connected?
- **Jot down negative words that have frequently popped into your head. Seeing them in print helps.**
- **Listen to the words coming out of your mouth.** You will learn a lot about yourself by paying attention to your spoken word even in prayer. Listen for words of comparison.
- **Practice thought tracking during your day.** Keep a written record or use an app. After a while, it becomes second nature.
- **Change the focus of your thoughts.** Said another way, think about something else. Anything else. As long as it is constructive.
- **Take responsibility for your thoughts.** No one makes you think anything.
- **Take your thoughts captive as soon as they pop into your head.** Create a temporary place for your thoughts. I often imagine a beautiful box (me and my boxes, huh?) at the feet of Jesus. I see myself dumping my thoughts in that box until later, while in the safety of His presence and during prayer, we open it together and examine its contents.
- **Memorize 2 Corinthians 2:5.** "And we take captive every thought to make it obedient to Christ."
- **Eliminate certain words from your vocabulary.** Any word that is unwholesome should be eliminated from your vocabulary—words that derogatively describe someone or something. You know what they are. They serve no useful purpose.

- **Pay attention to your inflection.** People can say the right words in all the wrong ways. It's just a way to say what they're thinking without using the actual unkind words. Same applies to you.
- **Pick a word you can concentrate on for the day.** The words *peace*, *joy*, and *calm* can soothe your emotions. Words like *focus* and *concentrate* can keep you on track. Words like *energize* and *determination* can get you moving.

The Environment Tools

- **If possible, reduce noise that makes you feel anxious.** This may be easier said than done.
- **Play music you enjoy.** It doesn't matter what style.
- **Increase the light in your home during winter by keeping shades up and curtains open.** There are some good lights on Amazon for depression called "Happy lights."
- **Make your environment smell good.** Use candles, potpourri, plants, even an open bottle of vanilla extract. Peppermint is invigorating, and lavender is calming.
- **Reduce clutter.** Find a place for everything. You can change it later if it's not right, but for right now, give it a home. There are tons of books about ways to manage clutter. Even though I was not a fan of Marie Kondo's method, I have since learned to appreciate it.
- **Clean up your space before bed.** Your mood will be much better the next day if you wake up to a neat house.
- **Build some structure** and organization into your life and your surroundings.

The Relationship Tools

- **Create a plan for dealing with people who discourage you or bring you down.** If you can, avoid

these people. If you can't, come up with a plan. There was a certain person I never talked to before noon because she was so irritable in the mornings.
- **Evaluate your friendships.** Which ones need improving? Which need to die a natural death? Be careful here. No long-term friendship should die easily.
- **Evaluate your role in your relationships.** What can you do better? Do you need to reach out more? Are you dependable? Can people count on you?
- **Examine the reciprocity in your relationships.** Does something need to change? Remember, don't make someone a priority in your life when you are just a passing thought in theirs.
- **Remember, not all the responsibility in a relationship depends on you.**
- **Make a list of who you are responsible for.** Make sure this is realistic.
- **Make a list of who you are not responsible for.** As above.
- **Compare the lists.** How do the lists compare? Is there some inequity? What can you do about it?
- **Forgive their failings.** We're all so human. Don't put family and friends on a pedestal. They will surely fall off. Don't let anyone put you on a pedestal either. You are bound to fall off as well.
- **Ask for forgiveness when needed.**
- **Give forgiveness when asked.**
- **Don't be overly sensitive.** (Talking to myself here.)

The Trigger Tools

- **Accurately acknowledge your feelings.** Don't lie to yourself. It doesn't help, and honesty prevents things from building up.

- **Express thankfulness out loud.** It keeps triggers at bay.
- **When you are feeling anxious, think back over your day.** Look for possible causes for any anger or tension you felt.
- **Track your moods daily.** Try to make a connection with your mood and what you were doing or thinking. Track on paper or an app.
- **If you can, avoid people and circumstances that cause you stress.** When you can't, have a plan for how, in the future, you can handle both the people and the circumstances. Just knowing you have some ideas in place will help you feel less stress. Stress can trigger anxiety, and anxiety can trigger depression.
- **Boredom can be a trigger.** Engage in something enjoyable every week. Have a list for when boredom strikes.
- **Develop a plan for social anxiety.** What can you plan ahead of time to make the next social situation not so anxiety producing? Like arriving early. Like picking out just one or two people to converse with.
- **Build some margin in your life.** Take stock of how much time you spend daily doing certain activities. Is there a way to streamline things?
- **Get enough quality sleep.** Schedule your bedtime and make sure everything you need to do is done that can be done ahead of time so you fall asleep and stay asleep.
- **Breathe properly.** Shallow breathing is a trigger.
- **Clean up the clutter.** Cluttered environments are a huge trigger.
- **Have a plan for sick days so you can keep your emotions in check.**

The Mood-Busting Tools

General

- **Accurately acknowledge your mood.** Don't sugarcoat it.
- **Accurately acknowledge your feelings.** Honesty prevents things from building up.
- **Make yourself presentable.** We always feel better when we are looking good. Look like a person someone would like to know.
- **Track your moods daily.** Try to make the connection between your mood and what you were doing or thinking. Trust me, there is always a connection.
- **Take your daily dose of vitamin G.** Remember, vitamin G is gratitude.
- **Smile.** Force the corners of your mouth to go up.
- **Reframe your emotions.** If you're angry about a person or a situation, don't ignore it, but reframe it so the sting is gone.
- **Pursue something you enjoy.** Even if it's only thirty minutes at a time, engage in something you really enjoy at least once a week if possible.
- **Examine your jealous feelings.**
- **Don't compare yourself to anyone unless it motivates you.**

Loneliness

- **Remember, God is always with you.** "It is the LORD who goes before you ... he will not leave you" (Deuteronomy 31:8).
- **Reach out to others.** There are others who are lonely too. Go find them.
- **Join an organization** to meet more people (church, book clubs, community groups, etc.).

- **Volunteer** for a good cause. It's a great way to meet people.
- **Reduce your expectations of others.** Other people can't always be expected to fill in for our loneliness.
- **Reduce your expectations of yourself.** It's OK to feel lonely at times. Don't expect so much of yourself.
- **Adopt a pet.**
- **House-sit a pet.**
- **Find others who share your interests.** There are so many ways to do that now.
- **Remember, being alone and being lonely are two different things**. Practice deliberate aloneness so you recognize the difference.

Anger

- **Admit your anger.** Who and what are you angry about? Make a list.
- **Make a list of people or circumstances you feel guilty about.** Something you did or didn't do.
- **Make a list of people or circumstances you are angry about.**
- **Compare the lists.** (This could prove eye-opening.) Which list plays the greatest role in your depression, your anger, or your feelings of guilt? You are only responsible for the guilt that is genuinely yours.
- **Ask for forgiveness if your anger has caused you to sin.**
- **Write your name on a slip of paper.** God has already forgiven you. Now, can you tear up that paper and throw it away? Unless you can, depression will never lose its hold on you.
- **Yell at a stuffed animal.**
- **Get help if your anger is disrupting your life or others'.**

Fear
- **Trust God to deliver you from your fear.** "I sought the Lord and he answered me; he delivered me from all my fears" (Psalm 34:4).
- **Admit your fear.** Remember, it's mentioned in more than two hundred verses in the Bible. Fear is obviously something God is aware of, which is why He has provided many verses for us to confront it.
- **Test your fear.** Does your fear have any basis in fact?
- **Confront your fear.** Don't be afraid to address it.
- **Pray your fear out loud.** There is no shame in fear and no fear you can't bring to God.
- **Breathe deeply.** Repeat throughout the day.
- **Walk or exercise.** Works for everything.
- **Distract yourself.** Works for everything.
- **Develop a plan for social gatherings if social anxiety is a problem for you.** Arrive early. Pick out just one or two people to converse with. Remember, you are probably not the only one feeling this way.

Anxiety
- **Trust God to see you through your anxiety.** "When anxiety was great within me, your consolation brought me joy" (Psalm 94:19).
- **Acknowledge you are anxious.** Again, you are not hiding anything from God. He can handle it.
- **Try to determine a common theme for your anxiety.** Most people have specific issues they feel anxious about. Fear often triggers anxiety. Look at the tools for fear again.
- **Breathe deeply.** Hold your breath for a few seconds by inhaling through your nose. Let it out through your mouth as slowly as you can. It's a great anxiety reliever.

- **When you have time, think through your day.** What things on your schedule can you put on autopilot?
- **Walk it off.**
- **Distract yourself.**
- **Clean up the clutter.** Excess clutter exacerbates anxiety.
- **Buy a weighted blanket.** Weighted blankets (I love mine) are much like an adult version of swaddling. They've been used for children with disabilities for years to reduce levels of anxiety. Or just pile on a bunch of blankets.
- **Remind yourself this is temporary.** Anxiety almost always goes away when we take our minds off it. The fact that it does proves it is temporary.
- **Think about something else.** Easier said than done but totally doable and always works.
- **Learn some grounding techniques.** Search online for grounding techniques for anxiety. Some may sound hokey, but give them a try.
- **Memorize Philippian 4:6–7.**

Sadness

- **Remember, God understands sadness.** "All my longings lie open before you, LORD; my sighing is not hidden from you" (Psalm 38:9).
- **Acknowledge your sadness.** There are no medals for toughing it out.
- **Make a list of what you are feeling sad about.** Are these items based on reality? If they are, what can you do?
- **Seek out your friends.** They might be sad too.
- **Go somewhere there are people.** Just being around people can help.
- **Walk outside.** Nature is therapeutic for everyone.
- **Read or watch something funny.** This may seem trivial, but it breaks the cycle.

- **Reach out to someone else.** Sadness is universal. Can you send a card or a text?
- **List all the things you are grateful for.** It really does help. Once we actually list the things and people we are grateful for, our sadness diminishes.
- **Distraction, distraction, distraction.**

Bible Reading
- **Show up.** It starts by showing up, which means setting a time and place and then doing it.
- **Pick up your Bible.** It doesn't matter why you haven't in the past. Just do it now.
- **Ask God to help you understand.** Take notes and use tools if you want, like concordances, Bible dictionaries, and commentaries. There are hundreds of tools online. But if you want to just read for now, that's perfectly OK.
- **Start with the Gospels.** Matthew, Mark, Luke and John, or the Psalms is a good place to start. Use an online version if you don't have a Bible in your home.
- **Read a chapter at a time.** After some time, increase your reading to a few chapters at a time because it flows better. Honestly, it won't take more than a few minutes.
- **Write in your Bible if you want.** It's not sacrilege. I write in mine all the time.
- **Make it a regular habit.** Try to read a few minutes every day. Even if it's different time every day and even if you are scheduling it day by day. For now, it doesn't matter.
- **Keep it up.** Trust God to help you understand as best you can for now. I still don't understand a lot of it. Just don't give up.

Meditation (Another part of Bible study for when you are ready.)

- **Concentrate on a portion of scripture.** Read it over a few times. Do some thinking.
- **Read the cross-references.** This gives you further clarification.
- **Who is the scripture written to?** Is it written to only the Jewish nation? It helps to know.
- **What is the main message?** Is there a particular message you can apply to your own life?
- **How can I apply what I read to my life?** That's the whole point of reading and meditating—change. Change that brings us closer to God.
- **Pray using the portion of scripture you've just read.**

Prayer

- **Again, show up.** As with Bible study, if you don't plan to show up, you won't.
- **Start praying with whatever words come into your head.** If you need a suggestion, you might try "Dear God" or "Dear Jesus." Just like with Bible study, the reasons you haven't in the past don't matter in the present.
- **Establish a daily time if you can.** You can even schedule each day and time differently.
- **Develop your own method and routine.** Most Christians include confession and thankfulness. (My blog has free resources you can try.)
- **Find a private place to pray.** I know a mother with young children where the bathroom is her ideal place.
- **Trust God to meet you in prayer.** God not only hears your prayer; He meets you in prayer. He is actively involved in the process.

- **Give yourself time.** Don't judge your words, your requests, or the length of your prayers. If ever there was a no-guilt zone, prayer time is it.
- **Be honest. Hold nothing back.** God loves the prayer of an honest, sincere person.
- **Just start talking to God.** Have a conversation as if He were your best friend, because He is. The rest will come.
- **If you don't know where to begin, pray the Lord's Prayer.**

Tithing
- **Start small** if you need to and work up to 10 percent and beyond.
- **Put your giving to the test.** See if you even notice what you are giving.
- **Tithe your time and your talents** to those who need it.
- **Keep your giving to yourself.** This is strictly between you and God.
- **If married, tithe in agreement with your spouse.**
- **Tithe your time or talents.**
- **Be on the alert for the blessings** that will come your way. They won't necessarily be financial blessings either. But you will be blessed.

Silence and Solitude
- **Plan a time to be alone with God.** If you can do this quarterly, great. But some of you will be lucky to schedule one time a year. Try by planning well in advance.
- **Decide what your time will look like.** Maybe there's a particular issue you want to concentrate on, or a particular person.
- **Remember, it's silent.** No noise of any kind, although soft music without words might be OK.

- **Be alert for God's voice.** It won't be audible. (Lucky you, though, if it is.) Often it will be just an impression that won't go away.
- **Have paper and pencil ready to record your thoughts.** However, don't get caught up with this. This is not a class you're taking. Keep note-taking to a minimum. Maybe just a few highlights.
- **Have a plan for how you will move out of this time.** Don't do it abruptly. Have a transition in mind. I find opening my eyes and simply sitting quietly for a few minutes is good. Don't just pop up and immediately get into a busy routine.
- **Savor this experience** throughout the next few days because God will continue speaking.

Fasting
- **Schedule a day ahead of time.** This isn't something to be decided upon at the last minute, especially if you have family you are preparing meals for.
- **Decide what kind of fast it will be.** Skipping one meal for a week? A total fast? A fast that allows fruit or vegetable juice? There are many types of fasts. Don't fast more than a couple of days without talking to your doctor first.
- **Remember this is a spiritual fast.** Much like silence and solitude, it is generally practiced for special wisdom, for a person, for healing, for direction, or whatever you want it to be.
- **Don't tell anyone unless necessary.** Don't be like the Pharisees and make a big deal out of it just for show.
- **Be prayerful throughout the day.** Fasting is meant to be a spiritual experience.
- **Be alert for God's voice.** Give particular attention to that still, small voice of the Holy Spirit.

- **Have paper and pencil ready (or your phone) to make notes.** This is different from silence and solitude, so jotting down a few thoughts is fine.
- **Come out of your fast slowly by gradually adding food.** Don't indulge in a big meal right away.

DISTRACTION IDEAS (NO PARTICULAR ORDER)

- Make a list of anything you have ever enjoyed doing.
- If time and money were not an issue, what would you like to do? (Scale it down so it's doable now.)
- Move.
- Smile.
- Pray.
- Read your Bible.
- Make a list of everything you like to look at, like to learn about, and appeals to you in any way, from coffee to architecture. Make the list long! You will be surprised at how helpful this can be.
- What did you want to do as a child when you grew up?
- Cut out pictures from magazines of anything and everything that sparks an interest. Glue them on a board.
- Volunteer.
- Walk in the woods or a park.
- Walk outside in your neighborhood.
- Do something every day that you enjoy. (It can be anything that is constructive.)
- Draw circles. Fill them in however you want. Mandalas have been proven to be relaxing.
- Doodle. Very therapeutic. Lots of ideas on Pinterest.
- Paint something, anything—a vase, a piece of furniture.
- Paint a picture.
- Color in a coloring book.
- Read (a novel, a subject you know nothing about, etc.).

- Browse a bookstore or library.
- Dance.
- Listen to music.
- Sing.
- Read to a child, even over the phone.
- Learn a new skill.
- Learn macramé.
- Browse Pinterest (Pinterest.com So many ideas that will jumpstart your interest.
- Write a handwritten note to someone.
- Offer encouragement to someone.
- Make a heartfelt gift for someone.
- Make a list of things you can do for someone else.
- Do something for someone else.
- Say a prayer for someone.
- Call someone
- Text someone.
- Learn something new about a country you would like to visit.
- Learn something new about an animal you like.
- Learn something new about your favorite food.
- Learn something new about your state, city, etc.
- Learn something new about anything.
- Play Words with Friends or Scrabble on an app
- Watch a funny show.
- Cook or bake.
- Organize your recipes
- Go fishing.
- Plant something.
- Have tea or coffee in a pretty mug.
- Fix a pretty table setting.
- Buy some flowers or pick some flowering branches.
- Ski.
- Snowshoe.

- Build a snowman
- Knit, crochet, or sew. These activities are very relaxing.
- Buy some pretty scrapbook paper even if you don't "scrap"
- Buy a pretty piece of fabric even if you don't sew.
- Make your own greeting card
- Plan your menus
- Read a cookbook
- Go thrift shopping. Find something to repurpose, paint, etc.
- Rearrange your furniture.
- Give away something.
- Work in your garden.
- Take some photos.
- Organize the garage.
- Organize anything.
- Clean a closet or a drawer.
- Write something.
- Read poetry.
- Write poetry. (You don't know until you try.)
- Write a children's story would've have liked as a child. (As above.)
- Browse the library for ideas about hobbies.
- Read a children's book because of the beautiful illustrations.
- Get a book with beautiful artwork.
- Create a to-do list of activities you used to enjoy.
- Create a list of things you might want to do.
- Create a bucket list.
- Watch Planet Earth on the BBC network
- Look at art pictures online.
- Visit a nursing home when the pandemic is over
- Do something, **anything** (nondestructive, that is). Just distract yourself.